BETTER MANAGEMENT

MANAGEMENT

SIX PRINCIPLES
FOR LEADERS TO MAKE
MANAGEMENT THEIR
COMPETITIVE ADVANTAGE

LUKAS MICHEL

ADVANCE PRAISE

"This book is for those who practice management, not for those who talk about it. So many management books are full of what managers should do. They tell you why, sometimes what, but seldom how. That is fundamentally what managers want to know – how to implement changes and, crucially, in their context. Lukas Michel's latest book builds on his others and gives managers a framework for their context and the 'how' to implement the ideas. It's as much workbook as textbook, with plenty of thoughtful exercises. Even though well-researched, both in theory and in practice, it's an easy read. It should give managers renewed optimism that they can make their organizations able to thrive in a VUCA world."

Nick Hixson, CEO, Hixsons business enablers,
Bournemouth, UK

"Twenty years ago, Lukas found his purpose in optimizing people-centric management by establishing Management Insights AG. Living his beliefs, he still aims to push management to new levels and, after five expert books dealing with his well thought out and complex concept, his sixth book *Better Management* enables a newcomer to get familiar with the ideas behind it. Knowing Lukas for more than a decade, I am still impressed by his passion, ideas, and beliefs to develop and push the art of better management."

Michael Eckert, Director Project Management, Electronics,
Merck KGaA, Darmstadt, Germany

"It takes courage to rethink how we get things done, especially on the management or leadership side. Michel's new book gives a clear idea about our current reality in making businesses successful and the challenges we are facing with the digitalization and the changing nature of work; but, at the same time, he offers a gentle self-mentoring to turn traditional management into better management and a road map with what he called 'The six principles of better management.' This book will challenge your beliefs and open innovative ways to deliver results through people's talent."

Sergio Seanez, CEO, Foundamentality, Mexico City, Mexico

"Lukas Michel's new book *Better Management* provides every leader with compelling insights and tools and serves as a time-tested and validated blueprint that will help to shift an organization from activity-based leadership to true and sustainable organizational effectiveness.

"Michel's timing of his new book could not be better, given today's managers are in absolute crisis as they attempt to lead in this VUCA world. *Better Management* can be the effective antidote to this management dilemma.

"Having sustainable high levels of performance requires leaders and organizations to be agile, to finally recognize the true and dynamic capabilities of a people-centric workplace – an opportunity to embrace and to share power with team members versus holding power over them.

"*Better Management* sets the stage and provides the guidance for organizations to follow, such that they will experience the value of having inner explorers, where innovation, creativity, and collaboration become core to the achievement of sustainable competitive advantage."

Mark W Beliczky, President and CEO,
ProHome Holdings, LLC, New York, NY, USA

Published by
LID Publishing
An imprint of LID Business Media Ltd.
LABS House, 15–19 Bloomsbury Way,
London, WC1A 2TH, UK

info@lidpublishing.com
www.lidpublishing.com

A member of:

businesspublishersroundtable.com

Printed by Severn, Gloucester
ISBN: 978-1-911687-26-9
ISBN: 978-1-911687-27-6 (ebook)

Cover and page design: Caroline Li

BETTER
MANAGEMENT

SIX PRINCIPLES
FOR LEADERS TO MAKE
MANAGEMENT THEIR
COMPETITIVE ADVANTAGE

LUKAS MICHEL

MADRID | MEXICO CITY | LONDON
BUENOS AIRES | BOGOTA | SHANGHAI

CONTENTS

To my wife, Charleen, for her support.

FOREWORD

It was in the spring of 2000 when our new head of strategy called our team together. I had only been with the company a few years, while he'd had a stellar career in a company that had just been acquired by ours. He was English, unconventional, and had been given some freedom by the Executive Board to restructure the strategic direction. He also wanted to reorganize us as his core team. It wasn't a question of replacing people; his goal was to divide the tasks among us in such a way that they optimally matched our skills and potential. Basically a banal step but, nevertheless for us at that time, new and unfamiliar. At the end of our short workshop, we all had suitable tasks, exciting challenges and, above all, a great desire to get involved.

In retrospect, it was the first moment in my professional career that I would describe with a clear conscience as "people-centric." It was the first time I had to deal with one of the aspects and principles that make up *Better Management* and which, as I am now aware, make a real difference and give a significant competitive advantage.

In retrospect, it is also clear why he, and we, failed in this attempt at the time. We were too strongly embedded in the classical thinking and culture of our large corporation. New ideas and impulses and the ways we approached them were viewed with suspicion and rejected. Agility, adaptability, and flexibility were not desired. Collaboration and decision-making were organized in such a way that dealing with the informal sidelines was always better because it was more efficient and effective. Although working outside the system was rewarded, it was an absolute must to work through the processes formally and cleanly, and to adhere strictly to the rules and specifications. Working on two tracks was the rule.

Last but not least, we rarely, if ever, looked back. What and how something was done was not reflected nor reviewed. Processes were additionally established and rarely abolished.

The company was a prisoner and slave of its own modus operandi; its own time-honored way of doing things. This was a fatal situation in view of the challenges that were to come in the next few years.

So, despite an initial spark of hope, we were still light years away from working and living in a company in which it was easy to actively use our existing skills and potential, and to continue to develop in a contemporary and forward-looking way.

In the meantime, more than 20 years later, this group is also trying hard to improve working conditions. But more and more, new products and offerings are no longer enough to achieve the expectations and goals it has set itself. The shift from analogue to digital business models, which have fewer and fewer differentiating features and can be copied more and more easily, also brings little real potential for success or even growth.

For myself, 2011 was the time to start my own business; to start and thus be able to work on it myself, to find and develop new ways of leadership and management that enable companies to be more successful, more forward-looking and at the same time more humane to the (ever) "new normal" and the wider future.

Management is, as Gary Hamel says, the "most important social technology." Anyone who is not willing and able to actively incorporate it into developments as the basis for human performance and the will to achieve will find it increasingly difficult to keep up in the competition for customers, resources and employees. Those who do not succeed in recognizing their own blind spots and changing their perspective and orientation will hardly be able to cope in an increasingly digital, complex, dynamic environment. It is about the emergence of the interplay of all capabilities and potentials, the meaningful use of all resources and potentials. It is about a new energy for each individual and, above all, for the entire company.

This book invites you to learn about the six most important principles of better management and to reflect on your own view of them again and again. It gives the opportunity to look at the interaction in the company from new perspectives, to analyze and change it. It shows what can be done, where and, most importantly, why, to move systems. It is the beginning of a learning journey that ends with nothing less than a more human, successful, and forward-looking way of working and living together in your organization. Be the starting point of the change that will lead your company into the future.

Guido Bosbach
Founder & Owner of ZUKUNFTheute,
Wachtberg, Germany

PREFACE

Renowned scholar Henry Mintzberg has defined management as the art, science, and craft to get work done. If that's so, then management touches everyone, everywhere, anytime. Most of us perform some kind of work. That's why we need to care about management and what it does to people and organizations.

However, the evidence is mounting that traditional management based on control, change management and employee engagement – all well meant – has passed its better days. The problem is not with managers (mostly). It's with *management*. Management, as we know it, must retire. Traditional management based on efficiency and control is ineffective in a dynamic environment where knowledge work dominates. Nowadays, exploration, innovation, creativity, collaboration, and self-organization is required.

Why would anyone continue to perform annual budgeting when the business cycles have shortened to much less than a year? You would have to adjust your goals and those of your employees more often. If you don't, then you assume that people do exactly what they have been told to do and follow their signed performance contracts. Mediocrity would be the result.

I know that there are still thousands of corporations out there that keep their managers and employees busy every fall with cumbersome target setting, performance reviews and alignment meetings without adding any value to clients. That time is definitively up.

In today's fully disruptive and hyper-dynamic environment, management likely is the one and only competitive advantage left. Others dissolve fast through digitalization and new business models with entirely different economics.

But for management to be a competitive advantage, it must be Better Management. For managers, the new dynamics impose one clear imperative: Every organization must build the capability to change into its very structure. It must commit to creating a new response to its challenges. Like with Kaizen, it must weave continuous self-improvement into daily life. And every organization must learn to innovate by organizing it as a systematic process. All these musts require a high degree of decentralization and structures where decisions can be made quickly.

Better Management is *the* yardstick. Six levels of fitness reflect the criteria of competitive advantages and, therefore, set the standards for management with agile, people-centric, and dynamic features. Over the past ten years, we have used the formula with clients of all kinds around the globe.

Our research confirms that investments in Better Management pay off. Companies that have established agile, people-centric, and dynamic capabilities outperform others by a huge margin. A similar study by McKinsey (Aghina, et al. 2021) in May 2021 confirms that the impact of highly successful agile transformation on efficiency, customer satisfaction, employee engagement, and operational performance yields 30% higher performance.

And, once developed, these capabilities permeate the entire organization – deeply embedded into the culture of the organization. They are a true competitive advantage that is hard to copy. Every manager needs to worry about that.

Better Management purposely and heavily draws on my former books and duplicates several parts. It is the brief and compact executive summary that highlights the model, the process, the workbook, the application, and the expert guide for diagnostic mentoring. It is the book for the executives who invest their time and attention in Better Management. Soon, they will not be alone. *The Performance Triangle* (2013) serves as a repository for definitions. *Management Design* (2021, 3rd edition) is the workbook for executives and the facilitation guide with the canvas. *People-Centric Management* (2020) is the application for leaders to work *on* the system. Over the years, we have learned that the transformation to Better Management starts with oneself, the leader and manager in charge.

Agile by Choice (2021) helps those who have not been convinced yet to reach their tipping point. And *Diagnostic Mentoring* (2021) continues to serve the experts and certified diagnostic mentors.

There is a desperate need for Better Management. Real managers know that it is their task to change the way they lead people, how they organize themselves, and how they get work done. Better Management is every manager's primary job. The evidence is clear: for successful transformations, 10% of employees can make or break it, as not all in the organizations will embrace the new way – nor may it be necessary that the entire organization gets it. But leaders at every level, not just top managers, must buy into it as organizational value and competitive advantage. Business disruption is only possible with the help of leaders who have crossed the Rubicon to better (Lang and Rumsey, 2018).

Management plays an important role moving to Better Management (Crocitto and Youssef, 2003). The key to what needs to be fixed is what happens at the top of the organization (Denning, 2021). From using our diagnostic tool to measure management based on the criteria for competitive advantage, we have learned that managers are overconfident of their own management and tend to underestimate the management capability of their teams. It's called the Dunning-Kruger (2011) effect. But why guess if you can know?

The Better Management standards come with the following:
- **A work environment** where people engage and get work done.
- **A strategy** that clears expectations with **results** that keep promises and create value.
- **Management** that mobilizes resources with self-responsible people who make the client offering specific.
- **People** who unfold their potential and perform in ways that are hard to copy.
- An **operating system** to master higher challenges without shortcuts.
- A **toolbox** with systems for leaders to capture new opportunities that is deeply embedded in culture.

It is interesting to note that, in overviews of key innovations over the past 200 years, management is never mentioned as a radical innovation that gets the respective recognition. Andrew Hill (2021), the *Financial Times* management journalist, put it as follows: "Take any middle manager from 2011 or 1991 or even 1961, and he would still belong to a large corporation, have an office with a desk, is somewhere on the org chart, has an incentive plan, is part of the hierarchy, follows a bunch of sociopaths with high-sounding titles giving orders." One of the reasons for missing innovation is that 20th-century traditional management systems still work. Hierarchy offers structure in a complex world. Offices provide a hub for face-to-face interactions. But the systemic inertia is to blame for the slow pace of change. "Rigid hierarchies can become bloated, timid, complex, insular, arthritic and highly politicized," to quote Gary Hamel talking at a workshop held at the 2021 Global Drucker Forum in Vienna.

Better Management is true innovation. Perhaps it is less of a radical innovation than a next evolutionary step. For the last 20 years, diagnostic mentoring has become the benchmark for supporting businesses with better management. The diagnostic creates awareness, and the mentoring expedites learning throughout an organization. A dedicated diagnostic tool helps managers assess their managerial fitness. It is accessible through our website (management-insights.ch). You can use the reports in line with *Better Management*.

Part I identifies the operating system that works in times when everything changes. Part II outlines the six principles of *Better Management*. With Part III, you can engage in the design of management along these principles. Part IV helps managers craft their shift to Better Management. And, finally, Part V is about work *in* the system – how you can make Better Management work for you.

By reading the book, become aware of what Better Management can do for your life, for your people, and the organization you are responsible for. It will clear your mind for what you have to do to establish Better Management throughout your organization. And it will expedite your learning about Better Management such that it becomes your competitive advantage.

While you read through the book, you may want to capture your answers on the questions at the end of every chapter. Use the notepad in the appendix to collect your ideas. Share them with your team.

Let me know once you have reached the tipping point of no return. Be welcomed in the community of those who engage in Better Management to improve the world – one by one.

PART I

THE CHALLENGES OF THE DIGITAL ERA

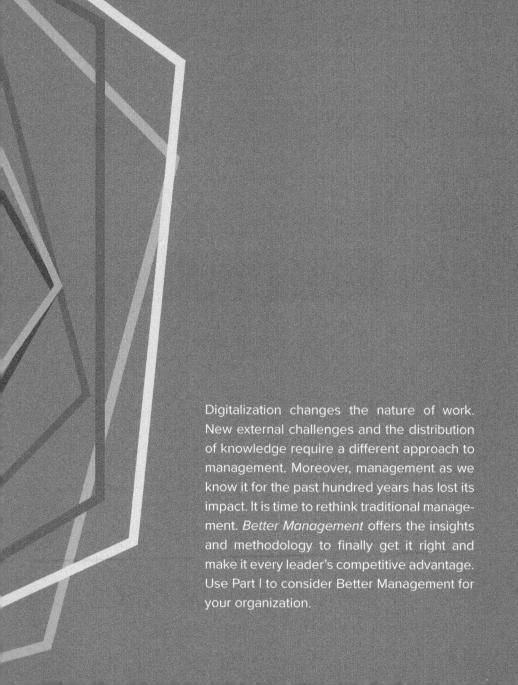

Digitalization changes the nature of work. New external challenges and the distribution of knowledge require a different approach to management. Moreover, management as we know it for the past hundred years has lost its impact. It is time to rethink traditional management. *Better Management* offers the insights and methodology to finally get it right and make it every leader's competitive advantage. Use Part I to consider Better Management for your organization.

CHAPTER
1

MANAGEMENT IN FLUX

Two trends – digitalization and the changing nature of work – fundamentally alter the way we manage people and organizations. New external challenges and more knowledge with people at the client front expedite the trend. Traditional control, change, and engagement-type management cannot cope with a digital context. Chapter 1 offers the capabilities-based management mode in response to these challenges.

THE NEW DIGITAL CONTEXT

Before diving into the *what* and the *how* of Better Management, it is essential to understand *why* management needs change. It's because businesses today operate in a context that is dramatically different from the past. Identifying valuable business opportunities and extracting value from them is more demanding than ever. Now is the time for a mind shift: rather than extract value, create value for customers.

Researchers and practitioners have observed that the rate of change caused by technology, globalization, and complexity has been increasing for years (Salmador and Bueno, 2007). The digitalization fundamentally changes the nature of work, how we organize, and how we lead people. Just about every company engages in digital transformation projects. But, to a large extent, the business and management remain the same. Businesses remain in the efficiency mode, whereas efficiency is becoming less and less effective. To address the opportunities of the future, businesses require a different operating model, one that scales learning. "In a rapidly changing world, the most powerful and necessary form of learning is learning in the form of creating new knowledge" (Hagel, 2021). Scalable learning helps expand the focus beyond efficiency. Knowledge is the primary resource for individuals and for the economy overall. The traditional production factors such as land, labour and capital become secondary (Drucker, 1992).

Digitalization lowers information costs and enables new forms of interaction. Today, information is readily available, large amounts of data can be processed quickly, and communication technologies enable remote work. With readily available information, organizations can gain new insights, capture opportunities early and promptly mitigate risks. The dramatic reduction of information-costs shifts work from being purely material and physical to something much more knowledge-oriented. Information search, knowledge creation and learning call for engaging the know-how and skills of remotely-situated people who are driven by self-determination and self-organization. Such decentralized, collaborative, and self-organized management styles are in sharp contrast with traditional approaches dominated by micromanagers.

When work requires the knowledge of employees, teams and communities, people-centric management dominates. In such modern contexts, formal 'control' approaches lose their function. Today's ease of communication permits management styles rooted in free choice, sharing, transparency and the absence of rigid structures. Such organizations must be organized for innovation and, as the Austro-American economist Joseph Schumpeter said, innovation seen as "creative destruction." The organization's function is to put knowledge to work. It needs to be organized for constant change.

Typical organizations and management are not invented to deal with rapid changes. Rigid hierarchies, organizational structures and information systems are not aligned with current needs, and corporate cultures resist new idea or processes. With increasing complexity, ambiguity, uncertainty and volatility, agile approaches are necessary to quickly adapt to the new environment (Murray and Greenes, 2006).

COMPLEXITY

Complexity increases with size. In established businesses, detailed home-grown processes and bureaucratic structures increase complexity. But as organizations grow and add complexity, the coordination of activities becomes increasingly important. Self-inflicted complexity is the result of more of everything, from the number of employees and operating locations to products on the shelf, segments served, functions performed and stakeholders with interests.

In a complex context, it is hard to understand – to hear weak signals, identify opportunities, and be clear about what matters – and to find purpose. But when we lack clarity, we ask for additional detail and more precise processes. We introduce additional bureaucracy, applying rules and coordinating procedures that work well in simple contexts. Complexity cannot be compacted. It cannot be addressed through methodologies. Self-organization through teams beats bureaucracy in complex contexts.

AMBIGUITY

Ambiguity requires choice. Rules of the game change, markets evolve, certainties dissolve, industries merge and change, loyalty vanishes, taboos are broken, and boundaries blur.

With increasing ambiguity, developing strategies and setting direction based on unpredictability and a variety of contextual settings requires information and knowledge. But when ambiguity creeps up, we set new rules and limit the degrees of freedom. We reinforce stability because we know how to deal with that. In ambiguous contexts, it is hard to decide – to select valuable opportunities and move in one direction. Relationships with those who know are needed. Ambiguity cannot be ruled and, in that context, delegation beats power. As such, seeing through ambiguity requires natural, team-based approaches as opposed to rational steps and simple models.

UNCERTAINTY

Uncertainty challenges strategy. Challenges to stability include shorter life cycles, less stable results, higher dependencies, more transparency, and higher reputation risks, particularly those that appear suddenly.

In an uncertain context, it's hard to act and collaborate (i.e., turn opportunities into benefits). The risks of failure are high. But when uncertainty rises, we second-guess ourselves, mistrust people, and limit delegation. We give orders and prevent the use of knowledge. In a stable, certain context, power and authority work well to get things done. Uncertainty cannot be controlled. But self-responsibility beats command and order. Digitalization helps decentralize decision-making without losing control. As such, uncertainty demands trusted management and nonlinear approaches.

VOLATILITY

Higher volatility is the norm in this day and age. Globalization, speed, real-time processes, faster decisions, synchronization, and immediate responses are required. In a highly dynamic context, flexibility is needed. Efficiency and scale require rigid routines for consistency and quality that work well in a stable context. But when control fails, we implement more of it. We double down with the tools and rein-force alignment. In a volatile environment, it's hard to maintain the focus on what truly matters, such as sticking with the opportunities. Narrow targets are always off. As such, attention beats detailed targets.

THE DISTRIBUTION OF KNOWLEDGE

Business is about exploiting valuable opportunities and turning them into client benefits. This requires information and knowledge: the second trigger. When knowledge is concentrated, control, command and central decision-making dominate. The speed of decisions and the flexibility for action depend on the ability to search for information and the available knowledge. Specialized knowledge is an appropriate response to a complex world (Lawrence and Lorsch, 1967).

The trend toward knowledge work has been widely documented by researchers and authors for decades. When knowledge is widely distributed, managers engage people to collaborate and connect to build relationships, all with a deep sense of purpose. Complex struc-tures are replaced by self-organized teams. They use inexpensive information and communications technologies in remote workplaces to detect opportunities early and act on weak market signals. With this, every organization has to build the management of change into its structure.

Information and knowledge to identify, select, transform and exploit valuable opportunities that benefit stakeholders are the best means to address the challenges of a VUCA (Volatility, Uncertainty, Complexity, Ambiguity) environment where knowledge is widely distributed.

People who are successful at constantly searching for and uncovering new opportunities generally know with clarity, move in one direction, mobilize their energy, and maintain their focus. With the knowledge worker generation entering managerial jobs, the distinction between managers and employees increasingly vanishes. To quote Drucker (2006), "With the knowledge age, employees become executives. They make decisions." This is why, for the purposes of this book, I often use 'people' to include leaders, managers, executives and employees.

The new context (Figure 1) distinguishes between traditional and agile. In a traditional context, leaders focus on evaluating transaction outcomes and how well employees adhere to organizational rules and processes. Traditional bureaucratic control approaches emphasize the specification, monitoring, and enforcement of rules and processes. Machines are good at efficiency and enable businesses to further exploit value.

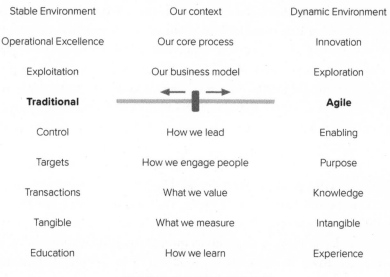

Stable Environment	Our context	Dynamic Environment
Operational Excellence	Our core process	Innovation
Exploitation	Our business model	Exploration
Traditional		**Agile**
Control	How we lead	Enabling
Targets	How we engage people	Purpose
Transactions	What we value	Knowledge
Tangible	What we measure	Intangible
Education	How we learn	Experience

FIGURE 1: THE NEW CONTEXT

Traditional organizations and management are barriers to achieving competitive advantage in a dynamic environment. Since many organizations today face a higher degree of VUCA, an operating model is needed that can deliver the expected outcomes amid ever-changing conditions. Traditional organizations were built for stability, efficiency and control. Centralized control and hierarchical structures are not suited to operate in fast-paced environments (Hugos, 2013).

With the dynamic context, the focus has shifted to faster learning and innovation. No company can control all the resources needed for innovation. Therefore, organizations increasingly need collaborative approaches, often with resources from outside the firm. As a consequence, they need to adapt their operating modes to the course, speed, and conditions of the external environment.

TRADITIONAL MANAGEMENT STRUGGLES

Traditional management is deeply embedded in the Anglo-American management mindset. The Harvard Business School's Chris Argyris calls practicing this mindset 'theory-in-use.' It is not the philosophical views that are expressed when you speak to managers. This predominant 'Cartesian' view – derived from the teachings of philosopher René Descartes – sees management as an engineering-like applied science, where the conscious mind and the actor (manager) are detached. His role is to rationally analyze, decide, and give practical instructions.

In traditional management, strict control procedures are used to cope with change and uncertainties. Hierarchies and vertical structures are established to create order. They are seen as a necessity for stability and planning. The general belief is that control is there to reduce risk. Employees are seen as interchangeable resources. Work is broken down in tasks that are allocated to people. Traditional management is based on control and command.

Many of the traditional management 'innovations' of the past failed because of this predominant mindset. It assumes and transcends an impoverished and inadequate view of humankind. The scholar and educator Sumantra Ghoshal (2005) called it the negative assumptions that underlie traditional management. Humans don't have one dominant mind. We have two minds that work together and play the inner game. In line with Gallwey's (2000) concept of the inner game, Self 1 is about the rational mind that makes judgments, gives commands and takes action. Self 2 is the human being himself, with all his potential and experience. Peak performance happens when Self 1 is quiet and Self 2 is in flow. Nothing interferes with the potential. Similarly, the psychologist and economist Daniel Kahnemann (2011) calls them System 1 and System 2. As he described it, System 1 is fast, automatic, active, and unconscious. System 2 is slow, tiring, aware, and logical.

The traditional 'division of the mind' offers left and right hemi-spheres. The left brain deals with the familiar, predictable, known, fixed, static, decontextualized, and explicit. The right brain is concerned with the novel, the possible, the unknown, variability, dynamics, the embedded, and the implicit. Philosophy suggests that the first brain (The Master) is existential. It handles questions like, "Who am I?" and "Why do I matter?" The second brain (His Emissary) is instrumental in dealing with questions like, "What do I want?" and "How do I get it?" Central to one's real-world function-ing is the relationship between the 'we' and the 'I' – the collective and the individual, soft and hard – which allows us to collaborate and to compete.

The prevailing scientific managerial mindset focuses on the rational, the known, the executive 'I' in pursuit of efficiency. As a result, people are treated as a means rather than an end. In that mindset, management innovations need to appeal to efficiency. This makes approaches with a focus on experience, awareness, the unknown, and the 'we' hard to sell. And we get more of the same efficiency – linear, mechanical, process-oriented.

The Cartesian view works well in the context of natural sciences. In management, its use is limited to a predictable context, when simple steps work, and where cause-and-effect relationships are stable. Such systems are simple. Rules and processes work well in that kind of context.

However, the Cartesian mindset does not work when it is applied to complex and dynamic systems where parameters are unstable, agents are interdependent, and cause-and-effect is non-linear. There is no manual for that. Dynamic contexts require an organic, ecological, adaptive approach. Things emerge, develop, and are nurtured and cultivated. It may be true that no two situ-ations are the same, but history matters. And experience is what puts things into habit.

People-centric has emerged from a different history, with a dif-ferent mindset. It's a mindset that is closely related to the humanist view of the world. Ghoshal (2008), whom we cited earlier regarding negative assumptions, would summarize this ethos as the set of positive assumptions that make up agile management.

Humanist management thinking that favours teamwork and collaboration through respect for people had its history, too. Its proponents have included the theorists Mary Parker Follett (1920s), Elton Mayo and Chester Barnard (1930s), Abraham Maslow (1940s), Douglas McGregor (1960s), Peter Drucker (1970s), Tom Peters and Robert Waterman (1980s), Jon Katzenbach and Douglas Smith (1990s), and Gary Hamel (2000s).

This formed the mindset and tradition that is deeply embedded in many European small and medium enterprises (SMEs), which have practiced agilely for the last 100 years, without naming or even being aware of it. Yet, despite almost a century of distinguished management writing, the truth is that the concept did not have a lasting impact on general management practice.

People-centric builds on a positive humanist tradition: Current reality helps people focus attention. Choice is freedom. Purpose is motivation. People are self-responsible.

Enabling, people-centric, agile, and dynamic models are well suited to it. With the goal of delighting customers, managers don't need to motivate employees to do the job. With managers and employees sharing the same goal – creating a customer – the humanistic, agile practices of awareness, choice, trust, and focus become not only possible but downright necessary.

Traditional management has lost its impact. Managers need alternatives on how to lead people and organizations.

THE CASE FOR A CAPABILITIES-BASED MANAGEMENT MODE

Management is in flux. Current reality shows that control, change and engagement have taken over management. Managers think that their job is to control work, manage change, or engage people. There are three failures of management that are apparent: traditional control, the change fallacy, and employee engagement. They all fail in the new business context.

Traditional control, with a focus on efficiency, has lost sight of people. Erroneous systems and faulty leadership are the cause. To overcome the challenges, well-intended managers compensate for the lack of leadership or workaround systems through their own 'pragmatic' solutions. I call this "working outside the system." Systems and leadership that are replaced by ad hoc interventions will lead to a virus-infected culture.

Change replaces management through sophisticated change processes and methodologies. The argument is that management systems and practices are not helpful for change, and that's why another process or methodology is needed. I call this "working with another system." Replacing management through change is not helpful. In fact, most change processes fail. Change management has failed.

Employee engagement cannot cope with a dynamic environment. While such initiatives search for better ways of working, they're merely what I would call a good attempt at "working with a better system." Why not simply update management with people-centric principles, rather than compensate for the apparent lack of good leadership?

The problem is not with managers. It is with the systems of control, change, and engagement. Control fails to work with knowledge workers. Change has long circled around management to bring about a different way of getting things done. Employee engagement has tried to change how we lead and work. None of that has worked well. The evidence is clear, and I have reported on this many times.

If the fault is with management, then that needs fixing. Distinguishing between operations (what managers want) and the operating systems (what most have not thought about) helps us emphasize where the true competitive advantage lies: the opportunity for real managers to think about how they lead, organize, and manage. That's work on the system. Real managers know that the task is to change the way we lead people, how we organize ourselves, and how we get work done. It's the primary responsibility of managers to establish an operating system that suits the people, the purpose of the organization, and the context of their business.

Four management modes (Figure 2) offer four bundles of managerial principles and capabilities.

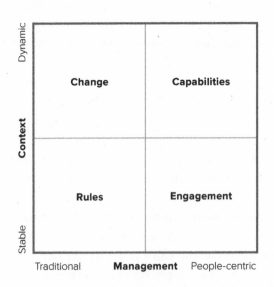

FIGURE 2: FOUR MANAGEMENT MODES

Here is a summary of the four modes:

Rules-based management works well in a stable context where the knowledge is concentrated at the top. Bureaucratic control procedures enable efficiency and help ensure the quality and reliability of products and services. People are here to follow orders. The rules-based mode is often combined with other modes in organizations that require a hybrid approach. A hospital emergency room is such an example. Teams normally follow standard procedures. When a special situation occurs, the staff's capabilities allow them to find creative solutions to the problem.

Engagement-based management works in knowledge-driven organizations that operate in a stable environment. Modern public administration of cities or states is a good example. People are encouraged to fully engage their talent.

Change-based management is favoured by companies that are highly regulated but need to frequently adapt their resource base to the changing environment. Financial services and the telecom sector are examples of industries that operate in this mode.

Capabilities-based management is preferred by businesses that favour a high degree of creativity and innovation. Start-up firms, research-based organizations and businesses in the exploration mode operate in this manner.

The shift to the capabilities-base mode is a shift to better management – beyond what traditional control, change and engagement can deliver in a fast-changing market context. In most organizations, the shift means a transformation of the operating system. Diagnostic mentoring offers the methodology for the transformation journey and serves as a guide for how to move beyond control, change, and engagement to better management.

Is your management in flux?
- Does your business face changes in the external environment and the way people work?
- Has your management lost impact in the digital context?
- Does your business face traditional control, endless change or weak employee engagement?

If your answers are yes, what can you do?
- Your management model and operating system likely need an update.
- Your business likely needs a people-centric, agile and dynamic management approach.
- You likely need better management based on capabilities.

Chapter 2 introduces the management operating system and what you can do to enable people perform at their peak.

MANAGEMENT IN FLUX

Management is in flux. Digitalization and VUCA challenges traditional ways to manage people and organizations. The capabilities-mode offers the alternative for managers to succeed when challenges rise.

KEY CHAPTER IDEAS

- The degree of external challenges and the distribution of knowledge require a rethink of management.
- The problem is not with managers, it's with *management*.
- Better Management comes with the capabilities-based management mode.

ACTION AGENDA

- Focus on Better Management. It's your primary job. Challenge current management and engage in the capabilities-based management mode.

FURTHER READING

Michel, L, Anzengruber, J, Wölfle, M, and Hixson, N (2018). Under What Conditions Do Rules-Based and Capability-Based Management Modes Dominate? Special Issue, *Risks in Financial and Real Estate Markets Journal*, 6 (32).

CHAPTER

2

THE OPERATING SYSTEM

Better Management comes with an operating system that is designed for the capabilities-based management mode. The Performance Triangle offers the elements that establish these capabilities. Peak performance is the goal. The task is to limit interference in ways that helps people unlock their full potential.

ENABLING PEOPLE TO ENGAGE AND PERFORM

In any organization, management operates on a system (Figure 3) that enables people to get work done. Such a managerial operating system facilitates interactions and creates a shared way of doing things. Think of the operating system in a computer: it makes the hardware work, enabling users to perform their tasks. In that sense, the managerial operating system does the same with organizations and people, through control, enabling, governance, and support.

Operations encompasses business transactions, how work is carried out through core competencies, processes, workflow, and output. The business model determines the nature of processes and work. Change in the business model means change in operations, the core processes, and how we operate our business.

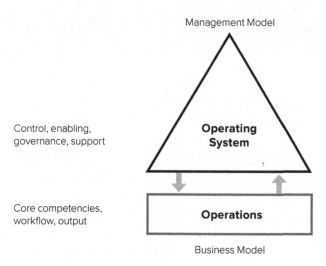

FIGURE 3: THE OPERATING SYSTEM

The operating system – the system of how we manage – is deeper and less visible. It is governed by the management model that deter-mines how we manage, lead, organize, and operate through culture, leadership, and systems. The operating system determines how we measure success, create strategy, implement plans, reward performance, and govern the decision-making.

The Performance Triangle (Figure 4) represents the managerial operating system (with rules, routines, and tools) to facilitate leadership and support people (with interaction skills). It also helps establish a shared culture (mindset), be it for one's own firm, organization, unit, or team, or as part of a farther-flung network, community, larger firm, organization, unit, or team.

FIGURE 4: THE PERFORMANCE TRIANGLE

The triangle establishes performance through operations that facilitate learning as an opportunity, a capability, and a state of readiness. The systems scientist Peter Senge (1990) put it as follows: "In a learning organization, leaders are designers, stewards, and teachers. They are responsible for building organizations where people continually expand their capabilities to understand complexity, clarify vision, and improve shared mental models – that is, they are responsible for learning."

An organization's operating system needs to establish the opportunity to learn. It's the responsibility of the organization to offer the learning opportunity. An employee's skills are the prerequisite for the ability to learn. The role of leadership is to unlock the talent; the goal is to engage the capability to perform. It's a shared responsibility between the organization and the individual.

The mindset is a prerequisite for the ability to act. It enables learning and the application of skills. Culture creates the context for readiness. But it's every individual's responsibility to learn and engage, and to remain in a state of readiness.

Operating systems have been increasingly challenged. Trust in systems is breaking down. And this is not unique to business – it's happening everywhere. More often than not, current discussions in politics and business challenge systems. We see political campaigns in modern democracies where candidates propose that public administration systems be torn down, claiming they aren't effective, are too expensive, have too many rules, limit freedom, and more.

Thousands of books are written every year that claim to add yet another attribute to leadership. They promise to provide 'the key to success,' 'the five recipes,' 'the ultimate goal,' and so on. Leadership without systems does not work. Systems without leadership are meaningless. And systems without the right design by their managers don't effectively support leadership and people. The Catholic priest and management author Peter Scholtes (1998) put it this way: "Changing the system will change what people do. Changing what people do will not change the system. Yet because we don't understand systems, we act as though human errors were the primary cause of our problems."

Culture matters. It embodies the set of formal and informal social norms in an organization. It is in the organization's interest to establish these norms in ways that enable people to cooperate in support of the overall performance goals. Culture provides what systems naturally cannot: the invisible, cooperative glue where targets, incentives, imperfect monitoring, and sanctions are based on the negative assumptions of people; and a solution to the 'free-ride' problem. One should not be surprised that cultures quickly turn sour and become infected by viruses (fear, control, and power).

We often see new CEOs demanding radical culture change, in hope of better performance and improved client service. This means there's a need for a new and different system to scale and govern decision-making, actions, and behaviours throughout an organization. A collaborative culture starts with positive assumptions about people, dynamic systems built in support of people, and people-centric management.

Every organization needs its operating system to ensure effective business conduct. The general critique that questions the need of systems per se is inadequate and misses the point. If a car does not perform to expectation, nobody would challenge the essence of cars in general. We know from our research that most culture issues, faulty leadership, or subpar performance originates from an erroneous operating system. If something produces errors, it needs to be fixed or exchanged. The critique, properly addressed, may demand a reset, an update, a change, or wholesale replacement of an organization's operating system.

Adaptive organizations need enabling leadership (Bäcklander, 2019). It's up to managers to build organizations where people can reach their full potential and be creative. Interactive leadership is an important tool for creating a work environment where people feel comfortable and satisfied with themselves and their work (Nold and Michel, 2016).

The operating system for the new capabilities-based context has a design that enables better management. It integrates the natural divide of the individual and the institution.

A SCHISM

So far in *Better Management*, we have discussed the need for a new operating system. Now, it is time to separate the individual and the institution for a better understanding of what is needed with the capabilities-based management mode.

Today's work requires collaboration and cooperation. As most work involves more than one person, we need to expand our view beyond people and managers. Instead, we should reimagine them all as executives who make decisions in today's knowledge era. To continue the conversation about Better Management and discuss management modes, we need to introduce a schism: a critical juncture that splits the executive into leadership (the individual) and systems (the institution).

Executives do not operate in isolation. They work with their management teams, lead people and worry about the functioning of their organization. While 'work in the system' is the focus of the *People-Centric Management* book, *Diagnostic Mentoring* turns to 'work on the system' and the need for people-centricity and agility in a dynamic context. *Better Management* features the capabilities needed for the digital era.

The Individual: Leadership	The Institution: Systems
The glass is half full or half empty	The glass may need to be twice as big
Work *in* the system	Work *on* the system
People development	Dynamic systems development
Heroic view: leaders as heroes	Post-heroic view: collective minds
Hard: can hardly be changed	Soft: can be changed (contrary to popular belief)
Source of people-centric thinking	The condition that creates the opportunity

FIGURE 5: THE INDIVIDUAL AND THE INSTITUTION

Figure 5 splits the idea of a single executive into a dualistic view of the individual and the institution. This schism helps us further dig into the sources of people-centric thinking, while at the same time talking about the conditions required to apply Better Management. As an executive, you have the duty and right (accountability/responsibility) to shape your conditions and those of every individual in your organization.

But, beware: in conflict, the institution always wins. System defects are always personalized. The dramaturgy of failure is always the same. Step 1: People note an institutional interference or error (the 'what is'). Then, Step 2 kicks in. The error falls back on the individual (this is the 'what should be'). That's why you should simultaneously care about leadership and systems.

We cannot discuss the institution, operating systems, and work on the system without a deep understanding of the individual and how they impact design. This is why we first turn to the individual.

Separating the individual and the institution is a deliberate Better Management action to dig into the foundations of the enabling capabilities-based operating environment.

THE INDIVIDUAL

Individuals play the inner game to cope with the challenges of the outer game (Figure 6). They make decisions: understand, think, act, engage, and adhere. They accept responsibility and are accountable for their results. They source their motivation from a combination of individual responsibility and the opportunities and systems offered by the institution.

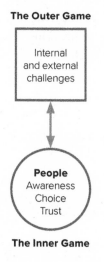

FIGURE 6: THE INDIVIDUAL

To capture relevant opportunities, people must deal with the personal challenges (the inner game) and external challenges (the outer game) they've set out to tackle (Gallwey, 2000). This bridges the outer game to the inner game of work. In that sense, the outer game represents the internal and external challenges people face when they perform. The bridge is needed to ensure that minimal interference occurs from the individual and the organization. Interference limits potential and reduces overall performance. Individuals – people – are the centre of attention in Better Management. The goal is to create a work environment that enables people to perform at their peak.

Peak performance is a reinforcing loop (Figure 7). With little interference, people can unlock their talents to take on greater challenges. With this, they reach the flow zone, where performance is at its peak. That fuels their ability to play the inner game even better, which closes and reinforces the performance loop. When people apply their inner game techniques, they have full access to their talents and skills. The inner game helps them better deal with internal and external interference and address greater challenges. These are the conditions where flow occurs; one arrives at the state where skills and challenges match. Staying in the flow zone requires people to continue applying and refining their inner game techniques. The positive reinforcing loop ('R' in Figure 7) closes, with better performance as the result.

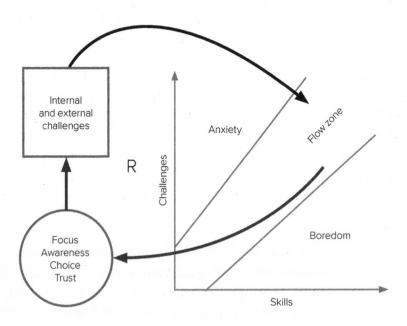

FIGURE 7: THE INDIVIDUAL PERFORMANCE LOOP

When anxiety or boredom prevail (internal challenges) or external challenges interfere, the loop turns negative and reinforces itself. In the context of greater internal and external challenges, it is more difficult to apply the inner game techniques. As a result, people can't apply their skills or challenges or may appear too formidable. Both effects prevent people from reaching the flow zone. The negative reinforcing loop closes, with poorer performance as the result.

There's a critical tipping point between the positive and the negative loop. The positive loop keeps us out of anxiety and boredom. It requires little interference and provides conditions where the potential can be applied. With the negative loop, interference prevents the talent from applying its potential.

Two conditions help individuals fall into the negative loop trap: the inability to apply the inner game techniques and little interference from the external environment. The inner game technique is individual and many of the external factors are institutional. Positive and negative loops can be weak or strong. Often, we don't notice the weak loops. We can easily handle them with our daily routines. Big loops, especially the negatives, require professional attention.

Diagnostic mentoring makes the tipping points of stress and the performance loop visible, supports individuals' practice of the inner game, and develops the external organizational environment to facilitate the return to the positive loop.

THE INSTITUTION

Most work requires more than one participant. That's why we need institutions. Institutions come as organizations that serve different purposes and are driven by different motives. Figure 8 bridges the institution's operating system and the context at work to show the challenges of the outer game that people and the institution accept. "The greater the external challenges accepted by a company, team or individual, the more important it is that there is minimum interference occurring from within," explained Gallwey (2000). In this light, the job of the leader is to create a work environment that limits interference. But, Gallwey added, "Resistance to change within the corporation is rooted in the prevailing command and control of corporate culture" (Gallwey, 2000).

For the individual to perform well, the institution's operating system and management must have a design that fits the challenges of the institution. The ideal design for significant challenges is the capabilities-based mode. The institution can perform effectively, innovation takes place, and it grows. The operating system and the ability to deal with the challenges create a reinforcing loop that delivers performance, innovation and growth.

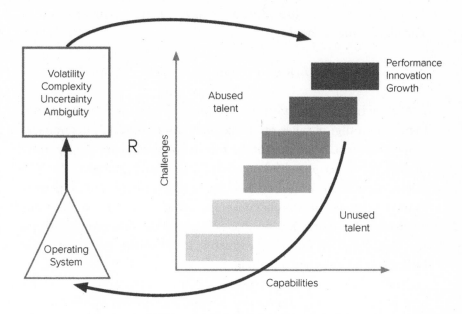

FIGURE 8: THE INSITUTIONAL PERFORMANCE LOOP

For the institution, the flow zone corresponds to management fitness, a concept that will be discussed in Chapter 14. The Better Management competency model indicates increasing levels of capabilities to deal with challenges. They are indicative of higher levels of performance, innovation, and growth.

When the institution operates in a control mode, it is unable to deal with a dynamic context. As a result, capabilities are unused and the operation delivers mediocre performance, little innovation, and no growth. In a work environment with little interference, the operating system helps people unfold their potential, with performance, innovation, and growth as the results. The enabling capabilities-based mode presents the characteristics of an operating system with little interference, where people can exercise their full potential.

That's why a large part of *Better Management* focuses on understanding the potential and the design of management and organization that minimizes interference. An enabling capabilities-based operating environment is designed to minimize interference and focus on supporting people's potential.

In 2000, Gallwey introduced a simple but powerful formula in *The Inner Game of Work*:

PERFORMANCE = POTENTIAL - INTERFERENCES

Leaders who manage with an operating system designed for analogue when digital takes over face daily interferences. This impacts employees, too, with mounting interferences and missing performance. When people with knowledge cannot engage and apply their talent, their talent is unused, and the business misses out on performance. With an interference-free operating system, people can put their talent to work. Knowledge is a capability that grows with its use. Engaging that knowledge must be in the interest of leaders, the business, and all other stakeholders.

The risks of 'business as usual' are substantial and can include lack of performance, unengaged people, and missed opportunities. And this is regardless of whether businesses operate in a stable environment or a dynamic one. The solution is to have a managerial operating system without viruses, where people can unlock their talent to deliver sustainable performance – consistently, reliably, and robustly – with agile features.

Does your operating system enable people to unlock their talents and perform at their peak?
- Do you and your people miss or fail to capture growth opportunities?
- Does anxiety or boredom keep people from performing?

If your answers are yes, what can you do?
- Your operating system needs an update or a full overhaul.
- Review your organization's operating system.

Chapter 3 introduces barriers to performance and the agile, people-centric and dynamic features that make your management better.

THE OPERATING SYSTEMS

Better Management with a capabilities-based operating system relies on an operating system that limits interference and helps people to unlock their talents.

KEY CHAPTER IDEAS

- The Performance Triangle offers the elements of an organization's operating system.
- Individuals play the inner and outer game to capture relevant opportunities.
- The operating system needs to ensure that there is minimum interference occurring from within the organization.

ACTION AGENDA

- Diagnose your organization's operating system to understand whether it supports good management or not. Spot the areas that require a fix.

FURTHER READING

Nold, H, Anzengruber, J, Michel, L, & Wolfle, M (2018). Organizational Agility: Testing Validity and Reliability of a Diagnostic Instrument. *Journal of Organizational Psychology*, 18 (3).

THREE FEATURES OF BETTER MANAGEMENT

Agile, people-centric, and dynamic are the three features of Better Management that help limit interference and unlock the potential of people. They keep the positive performance loop going. Better Management reduces the interference.

THE POSITIVE
PERFORMANCE LOOP

With little interference from the institution and themselves, individuals operate in the flow zone and perform at their peak. Consequently, the institution gets work done, resulting in performance, innovation and growth. Figure 9 shows the reinforcing loops between the individual and the institution. The operating system establishes a work environment that facilitates the application of inner game techniques. As such, the individual is able to deal with greater challenges. The positive performance loop dominates.

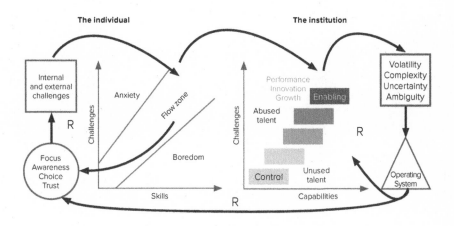

FIGURE 9: THE POSITIVE PERFORMANCE LOOP

If, for various reasons, the operating system is infected, the institution's balance of capabilities and challenges is compromised. Individuals feel that their talent gets abused. The operating system has a design that forces leaders to put pressure on people without respecting current capabilities. Pressure creates stress and diminishes performance. Pressure also leads to anxiety. People are afraid to expose themselves or tackle challenges that involve risks. With pressure, internal and external challenges grow, which makes it more difficult for people to apply the inner game –s the techniques that bring about peak performance. At worst, people mentally, and perhaps even physically, resign. Getting out of the context of a toxic culture, flawed leadership, or broken systems is a much greater challenge than making sure that the negative spiral does not begin in the first place.

WHEN VIRUSES CREEP INTO THE ORGANIZATION

When viruses creep into an organization, it is time for spring cleaning. These viruses might take the form of a toxic culture, flawed leadership, or broken systems.

Toxic culture: Examples include faulty operating procedures, business values that are not clearly linked to outcomes, cynicism, upward delegation, outdated reasons for centralized decision-making, a technocratic view of decision-making, and a lack of shared assumptions. Culture is one of the things that gets the blame. But culture is an outcome – it's a feature that cannot be changed directly. A toxic culture creates subtle dissonances that are hard to detect. Fixing culture requires altering systems and leadership through workshops, mentoring, and/or corporate programmes that are well-crafted and professionally orchestrated. A defective culture's roots always lie in flawed leadership or broken systems. So, the task is to fix leadership or systems first.

Flawed leadership: Examples include excessive control, busyness, lack of time, disproportionate attention to detail, senselessness, obsessive focus on numbers, and minimal added value. Normally, organizations hire the best and train them to stay that way or to fit given templates. Bad leadership normally comes in counts of one. If otherwise, we have a different problem for which the only fix is replacement of an entire leadership team. As such, the flaw can be located and isolated, as it normally resides with one person (or a small group of them). Replacing a leader is an option, but it normally comes too late. And viruses spread. An immediate reaction is evident. Fixing a leader takes time, and toxins might still spread for a while. It is expensive and the likelihood of success is questionable, despite the promises of a huge 'leadership-fixing' industry. Coaching or training flawed leaders is ineffective. Performance problems can be fixed where there is a will to learn. Behavioural problems (or a mixture of performance and behavioural problems) require a different course of action.

Broken systems: Examples include bureaucratic or nonexistent routines, formalism, faulty design, revisiting past decisions, slow implementation that hampers decision-making, rules infected with the 'viruses,' and ineffective tools. Normally, it is a specific set of systems that cause flawed leadership. Common culprits include management by objectives, incentives, budgeting, resource allocation, and communications. When any of these is broken, it affects the entire organization. Systems viruses have huge leverage. Human resources, financial officers, risk officers, governance officers, and all other support officers are often the cause rather than a symptom. They may be individually optimized but not aligned. Fixing systems is critical and affects the entire organization, so it is often a risk. But not doing anything is not an option. It is comparatively cheap to fix broken systems. It is a free choice, and it can be done quickly. Yet, simply fixing the toolbox might not be good enough. It might require a new design, for example, to fundamentally rethink the way you lead the organization. The symptoms of a broken operating system are everywhere. The causes often lie with the tools, routines or rules that govern the prevailing management model. All of these are signs of a toxic culture that's missing energy or is lacking in flow experiences. The result is crippled creativity and stagnation.

Diagnostic mentoring decodes these viruses, designs Better Management and healthy organizations, and installs an operating system that supports peak performance throughout the institution. The enabling work environment limits interference – it removes a toxic culture, flawed leadership, and broken systems.

THREE ECOSYSTEMS

For management to perform at a high level of fitness and organizations to operate at agile maturity in a challenging market context, three capabilities are needed (Figure 10):

- **People-centric management** (*People-Centric Management*, Michel, 2020)
- **Agile organization** (*The Performance Triangle*, Michel, 2013)
- **Dynamic operating system** (*Management Design*, Michel, 2021, 3rd ed.)

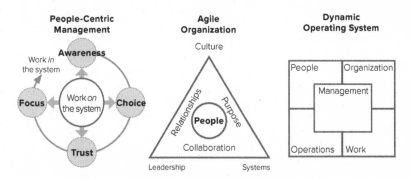

Being people-centric is a necessary management attribute if an organization is to benefit from talented people who possess skills, knowledge, and a high-performance attitude. People-centric management follows the principles of self-responsibility, delegation, self-organization, and focus of attention. Such enabling management is in sharp contrast to traditional management, where authoritarian control and command prevail.

The people-centric ecosystem (Figure 11) consists of enabling systems and supporting leadership that function as a positive loop, with sufficient resources to balance out the ecosystem. Leadership and systems enable people to apply inner-game techniques that allow them to fully use their talent. With an enabling environment, people are able to face down ever-greater challenges. The reinforcing loop sets in. The toolbox of resources ensures that the positive or negative reinforcing loop remains within limits.

Work *in* the system aims to support both the reinforcing and the balancing loop. People-centric leaders work with systems that help people quiet their minds, fully apply their capabilities, and use their resources wisely. People-centric management means responsible leadership and supportive systems.

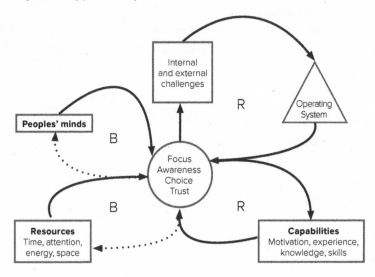

FIGURE 11: THE PEOPLE-CENTRIC ECOSYSTEM

As such, people-centric management requires work on the system. That work consists of making sure systems and leadership meet the needs of people, helping them play the inner game – dealing with their active minds and ensuring the effective use of resources and capabilities. Effective use implies the productive utilization of time, attention, energy, and space. Doing this all effectively also means that there's room (and budget) to refuel limited resources. Doing this will help build the organization's stores of experience, knowledge, and skills.

Agile is the necessary feature of organizations in support of people-centric management (Figure 12). Agile creates a work environment where people serve their customers in ways that generate positive returns for the organization and its stakeholders.

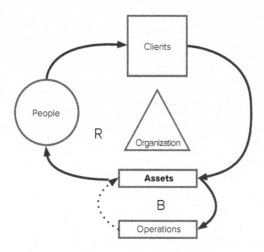

FIGURE 12: THE AGILE ECOSYSTEM

The agile ecosystem consists of an organization with a shared culture, interactive leadership, and an effective operating system. Managers use the operating system to make investment decisions on assets and human resources. People with the right talents satisfy customers, who ultimately come back and want more. Returning customers add to the growth of assets that can then be reinvested. Organizations with the right operating systems have assets that require investments. Agile means that there is a shared culture, interactive leadership, and a supportive operating system. None of these three elements come for free. The need to continuously invest balances the reinforcing loop of organizations that nurture customers who come back.

Dynamic is the feature of operating systems that enables people to cope with the challenges of VUCA (Figure 13). The ability of people, the organization, work, operations, and management to address a challenging environment better than the competition drives growth and considerably reduces costs and operational risks.

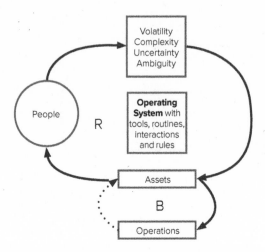

FIGURE 13: THE DYNAMIC ECOSYSTEM

The dynamic feature of an operating ecosystem consists of rules, routines and tools that facilitate interactive leadership. Meaningful interactions and the diagnostic feature of systems enable people to deal with greater challenges. Such operating systems with dynamic features come with tools that can handle volatility, routines that deal with complexity, interactions for uncertainty, and rules for dealing with ambiguity. The dynamic features of an operating system require the specific design of the rules, routines, tools, and interactions. Design is a deliberate investment in an operating system that enables people, the organization, work, operations, and management to handle adversity better than others. And that is a true competitive advantage.

In a people-centric, agile, and dynamic operating context, people can reach their flow state more often without interference from their minds and 'the organization.' They can play the inner game and perform at their peak with the outer game. That operating context comes with a high level of managerial fitness, agile maturity throughout the organization, and the dynamic features of the operating systems. Making it so is a deliberate choice every manager has to make.

People-centric, agile, and dynamic are the features of an enabling operating environment. Diagnostic mentoring ensures that these features become part of Better Management.

Does your operating system keep people from engaging their full talent?

- Do you miss agile, people-centric and dynamic capabilities?
- Do you observe a toxic culture, flawed leadership, or broken systems?

If your answers are yes, what can you do?

- Consider developing these capabilities.

Chapter 4 introduces business models and how to match the management model in ways that favour Better Management.

THREE FEATURES OF BETTER MANAGEMENT

People-centric, agile, and dynamic are the features of Better Management. Their purpose is to enable the organization to deal with a dynamic context and people to capture higher challenges by limiting interference.

KEY CHAPTER IDEAS

- People-centric is about enabling people rather than controlling them.
- Agile makes the organization flexible and adaptable to change.
- Dynamic is the feature of operating systems that enables people to deal with external challenges.

ACTION AGENDA

- Use the diagnostic to review and develop these capabilities.

FURTHER READING

Michel, L (2021). *Management Design: Managing People and Organizations in Turbulent Times* (Third ed.). London: LID Publishing.

Nold, H & Michel, L (2016). The Performance Triangle: A Model for Corporate Agility. *Leadership & Organizational Development Journal*, 37 (3).

CHAPTER

4

BETTER MANAGEMENT FITS THE BUSINESS

Nine generic strategies offer the choice of an exploitation or exploration type of business model. Exploitation aligns well with traditional, rules-based management modes. Exploration requires a capabilities-based mode. The choice determines the design of the operating systems and what people do.

STRATEGY DETERMINES THE BUSINESS MODEL

The strategy determines your business and operating models, which mark the starting point of every agile journey. MIT academics Arnoldo Hax and Nicolas Majluf (1996) suggest nine distinct strategies that cover most businesses, whether they're start-ups, traditional organizations, platforms, or ecosystems of networked companies. The choices are presented in a table that aligns the positioning with a company's core processes. Figure 14 offers a choice of nine different business strategies to help you decide on your dominant strategy.

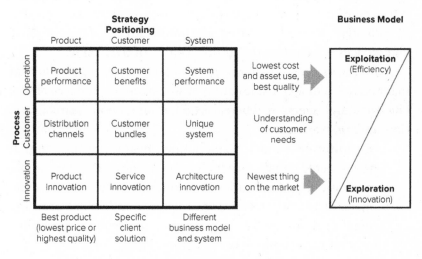

FIGURE 14: STRATEGY AND BUSINESS MODEL

The best product performance builds on traditional forms of competition. Customers are attracted by low cost or differentiation that introduces new features. Innovation is centred on internal product development. The 'total customer solution' strategy is the complete opposite of the 'best product' approach. Instead of commoditizing the customer, a deep understanding of the customer and the relationship is developed. An integrated supply chain links key suppliers and customers. Innovation is aimed at the joint development of distinctive products. The systems strategy includes the extended enterprise, with customers, suppliers, and complementors (companies whose product adds value to your offering) as a network, a platform, or an ecosystem. This relationship may span the entire value chain, from product to delivery. Distribution channels are a key consideration, as they involve ownership or restricting access.

Aligning the key activities with the three strategies follows three adaptive processes: operational effectiveness, customer targeting and innovation. Operations is about the manufacturing and delivery of products and services. It aims for the most effective use of assets, such as machines and infrastructure, to support the chosen strategic position of the company. Customer targeting is about the management of the customer interface. It should establish the best revenue infrastructure for the company. Innovation is about new product development. It should ensure a continuous stream of new products and services to maintain the future viability of the business.

With clarity on your strategy, you can now determine your dominant business model: exploitation business models concern choice, efficiency, and selection, whereas exploration is about search, variation, and innovation.

- **Exploitation model**: Exploitation includes such things as refinement, choice, production, efficiency, selection, implementation, and execution. Exploitation involves the refinement of existing technology, requiring individual coordination. Exploitation as a business model requires traditional control-based approaches to management.
- **Exploration model**: Exploration includes things captured by search, variation, risk taking, experimentation, play, flexibility, discovery, and innovation. Exploration is an adaptable and flexible process, which has to fit the new configuration the company pursues. It arises from individual deviation from the norm, as a source of innovation. Exploitation relies on innovation and requires a capabilities-based approach to management.
- **Hybrid/dual model:** Combining exploitation and exploration poses a dilemma, as they compete for the same scarce resources. The challenge is to combine both in a way that

guarantees the survival of the company – a trade-off between variation and selection, between change and stability. The combination delivers learning as a concurrent development and diffusion of knowledge throughout the organization.

Operational effectiveness is all about exploitation, whereas innovation relates to exploration. The hybrid model combines both exploitation and exploration.

BUSINESS MODEL AND MANAGEMENT MODE MUST MATCH

Business models and operating modes must match. Exploitation business models favour control approaches. Exploration business models demand enabling management. Hybrid business models often use change or engagement modes (Figure 15).

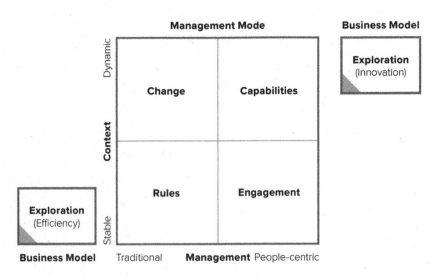

FIGURE 15: BUSINESS MODEL AND MANAGEMENT MODE

The dominant business model determines the dominant management mode, the operating systems and with this, what people do (Figure 16).

Business Model	Exploitation: Efficiency	Exploration: Innovation
Management Mode	Rules-based: Stable context, traditional management	Capabilities-based: Dynamic context, people-centric management
Operating System	Bureaucratic	Agile, people-centric, dynamic
People Performance	Follow orders and procedures	Are creative and capture opportunities

FIGURE 16: THE BUSINESS, THE INSTITUTION, AND THE INDIVIDUAL

Exploitation-type business models favour rules-based management modes for high efficiency. Their operating system enables traditional, bureaucratic management. With this, people follow orders and procedures. The result is reliability, predictability, and quality.

Exploration-type business models prefer capabilities-based management modes that enable innovation. Agile, people-centric and dynamic are the features of the operating system. The goal is that people are creative and capture growth opportunities.

The choice of the dominant business model has consequences for the management mode, the operating system and what people do.

Do you notice a mismatch between the business, management, the operating system and what people do? Neither efficiency nor innovation sets you apart from the competition?

- Does your organization miss opportunities or fail to deliver on its expectations?
- Are your people confused about what they should do and how to perform?

If your answers are yes, what can you do?

- You likely need to better align business, management, and operations.

Chapter 6 introduces management as a competitive advantage and why you should care about your operating system.

BETTER MANAGEMENT FITS THE BUSINESS

Better Management requires that your management model fits your business model.

KEY CHAPTER IDEAS

- Nine strategies determine the business model.
- Exploitation and exploration are two fundamental business model choices.
- Exploitation comes with a rules-based management mode.
- Exploration requires a capabilities-based management mode.
- The choice of your management mode determines the operating system.

ACTION AGENDA

- Align your management mode with your dominant business model.

FURTHER READING

Michel, L (2021). *Diagnostic Mentoring: How to Transform the Way We Manage*. London: LID Publishing.

CHAPTER

5

MANAGEMENT IS *THE* COMPETITIVE ADVANTAGE

Competitive advantage is at the heart of the performance of businesses in competitive markets. It's how a company puts its strategy to work through cost leadership, differentiation, and focus. The traditional domain of competitive advantage is on the value chain, the operations of a company.

In today's fully disruptive and hyper-dynamic global markets, traditional competitive advantages based on the value chain dissolve fast. New business models can quickly alter the cost position of a company. Business ecosystems can differentiate the value proposition in unprecedented ways. Globalization has turned narrow markets into huge markets permanently diluting focus. More than ever before, traditional competitive advantages based on the value chain are hard to maintain in ways that offers sustainable above-average returns.

The last remaining areas of competitive advantage can be found with management, the management model and the operating system of a company. Management is, in line with Porter's (1985) distinction, neither a primary activity nor a support activity. It is the activity that makes all other activities happen. Our research claims that management is one of the only remaining sustainable competitive advantages.

We claim that agile, people-centric, and dynamic features turn management into a competitive advantage. Performance, innovation, and growth are indicative for the returns of competitive advantages. Figure 17 relates competitive advantage, measured through the agile, people-centric, and dynamic features of management, with the returns of superior management, being outcomes measured through the performance, innovation, and growth of 400 companies of all kinds around the globe. The data clearly shows a strong correlation between capabilities and outcomes. It is indicative for a strong relationship of dynamic capabilities and business outcomes.

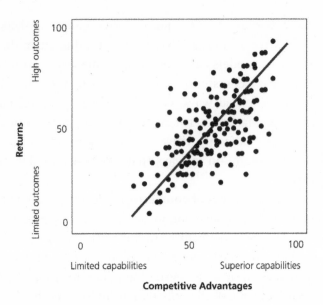

FIGURE 17: COMPETITIVE ADVANTAGE AND RETURNS

To be a true differentiator, management needs to fulfil the criteria of a competitive advantage. In line with strategic management professor Jay B Barney's resource-based view of the firm (1991) and the VRIN criteria for competitive advantage (valuable, rare, inimitable and nonsubstitutable), our research has identified a model with six features to signal whether management qualifies as a competitive advantage (Figure 18).

FIGURE 18: MANAGEMENT AS A COMPETITIVE ADVANTAGE

Management must fulfil all six criteria to qualify as a competitive advantage. The criteria and their components are as follows:

Does the work environment enable people to get work done? Our model uses culture, purpose, relationships, and collaboration to size up the work environment. An engaging work environment is a competitive advantage because it enables people to get work done.

Does your organization keep promises and create value? Our model uses performance, innovation, growth, and success to determine organizational outcomes and reveal whether management creates value. Keeping promises is a competitive advantage because it establishes trust with clients, which is of greatest value.

Does your management create unique value? Our model uses ten questions to review whether management applies a control-based (traditional management) or an enabling-based (people-centric management) approach to leading people. A people-centric management approach is a competitive advantage because it mobilizes resources in ways that make the client offering specific.

Do people use their talent to exceed expectations? Our model uses awareness, trust, choice, and focus of attention as the means for people to experience flow, perform at their peak and learn. Achieving flow more often – the state of high performance – is a competitive advantage that is hard to copy.

Is your operating system read for VUCA? Our model reviews the operating system to evaluate whether it has a design for a traditional or a dynamic environment. A dynamic operating system is a competitive advantage, as it prevents shortcuts.

Is your toolbox deeply embedded in culture? Our model looks at systems and leadership with interactive and diagnostic features. Their usage tells us whether the toolbox is rooted in the culture and is a competitive advantage.

With these six features, Better Management turns into a competitive advantage. Companies that have established agile, people-centric and dynamic capabilities outperform others by a huge margin. And, once developed, these capabilities permeate the entire organization – deeply embedded into the culture of the organization. They are a true competitive advantage that is hard to copy. That's why every manager needs to worry about Better Management.

Does your management not differ from that of competitors?

- Does management keep people from performing and applying their talents?
- Does your management primarily serve control and command?

If your answers are yes, what can you do?

- Your management has the potential to become better. Work at it.

In the following chapters that make up Part II of *Better Management*, we will investigate the details of every one of the six factors that make management a competitive advantage.

MANAGEMENT IS THE COMPETITIVE ADVANTAGE

Better management is one of the last remaining competitive advantages. Six elements help leaders diagnose and develop management for greater returns.

KEY CHAPTER IDEAS

1. Management is one of the few remaining competitive advantages.
2. People-centric, agile and dynamic are the features of better management.
3. Better management as a competitive advantage has higher returns as compared to traditional management.

ACTION AGENDA

- Review your management based on the six elements that make it a competitive advantage.

FURTHER READING

Michel, L (2021). *Diagnostic Mentoring: How to Transform the Way We Manage*. London: LID Publishing.

PART II

THE SIX PRINCIPLES OF BETTER MANAGEMENT

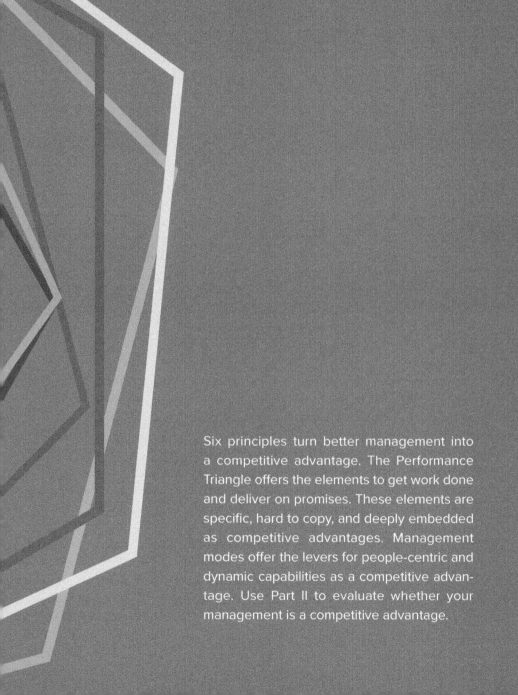

Six principles turn better management into a competitive advantage. The Performance Triangle offers the elements to get work done and deliver on promises. These elements are specific, hard to copy, and deeply embedded as competitive advantages. Management modes offer the levers for people-centric and dynamic capabilities as a competitive advantage. Use Part II to evaluate whether your management is a competitive advantage.

CHAPTER

6

VIRUS FREE

Principle #1, Virus free, means a work environment that offers the opportunity to engage and get work done. As such, culture, purpose, relationships, and collaboration are a competitive advantage.

Can people fully engage and get work done?

WORK ENVIRONMENT

Culture, leadership, and systems frame the corners of the triangle (Figure 19). Superior decision-making and effective actions require a culture that creates shared context. Culture works like an invisible compass. It embodies the values and norms around how to do things that people embrace: the shared understanding, intent, agenda, beliefs, and norms.

FIGURE 19: WORK ENVIRONMENT

Purpose, collaboration, and relationships represent the three sides of the Work Environment (Figure 19). People need three things to perform: to find purpose in what they do, collaborate with others, and connect with others to gain more knowledge.

Purpose, relationships, and collaboration are the bonding elements of every organization. For superior decisions, knowledge work requires purpose. It is the driving force behind motivation.

Knowledge workers use internal and external relationships to share and expand their knowledge, to create value for clients. Only knowledge that is shared and applied has value for any organization. New technologies facilitate the transfer of knowledge in a way that generates new knowledge.

Many knowledge-related tasks in an organization require more than one individual for their completion. It is the combined knowledge and the shared experiences of collaboration, connectivity, and purpose that stimulate people to get work done.

Culture is a key element that determines whether work gets done. The culture of an organization creates shared context, enables or inhibits knowledge exchange, and defines the invisible boundaries of collaboration. A vibrant culture establishes shared context as the common ground, with a mutual agenda, language, thought models, relationships, and purpose. Shared context is all about a shared mindset: the behaviour of individuals based on common thinking and shared norms. The organizational culture becomes the invisible force that, like gravity, shapes all interactions within the universe in which the organization exists.

We agree with the assertion that culture has both visible and invisible components, underlying beliefs, values, and shared assumptions that shape collective thoughts. They can be observed through the decisions, behaviours and actions of the people in the organization. Culture has a stabilizing effect on the organization and helps people make things meaningful and predictable.

It is important to note that changing culture is more than changing individual mindsets. It's about the collective behaviours as a sort of habit system. Such systems can only be changed by action, experience, and feedback, attained through experience, rather than the cognitive abstractions of new values. This is why culture is an outcome, with systems and leadership as its triggers.

These five culture elements, which establish a shared mindset, include:

1. Shared **understanding** to know with clarity.
2. Shared **intent** to move in one direction.
3. Shared **agenda** to mobilize the energy.
4. Shared **aspirations** to maintain the focus.
5. Shared **norms** to maintain the focus.

Purpose connects systems and cultures to people. However, as the philosopher and sociologist Jürgen Habermas said, "There is no administrative production of purpose" (1988). What we often hear when the climate changes is that when people lose sight of the purpose of their work, companies start a discussion on motivation. When people experience their work as meaningful, they contribute with greater energy. They're fully present – physically, mentally and emotionally. Purpose is created individually, subjectively. It is always 'me' who provides purpose to the world. It is called sense-making, not 'sense-giving.' Purpose cannot be delivered; it needs to be found or 'produced' individually. Individuals search for purpose. But, in tough times, purpose needs reinforcement. Agile techniques enable purpose at scale.

Relationships are the cornerstones of every business transaction. In individualized, people-to-people business relationships with external stakeholders, trust and agreement between employees and the organization are essential. As such, 'relationship capital' is essential to the value of a company. But good relationships come at a price. They impose a challenge on every leader of an organization. Relationships also relate to interpersonal connectivity. The greater the number of connections among people in an organization, the more restrictions and boundaries they place on one another. This limits their freedom of movement and their ability to perform. As a result, relationships and connectivity must be tuned to the optimum level.

Relationships are an important means for addressing the challenges in an ambiguous context. Connected people with diverse knowledge make better decisions in any context, and with a variety of outcomes, than one lonely manager might. Individuals connect and build relationships. Agile techniques enable relationships at scale.

Collaboration is an issue because of complexity, which increases with size and scope. We keep adding functions, geographies, departments, services, client groups, and other structures to our organizations. In a complex and networked world where knowledge matters, collaboration is more important than ever. Every structure creates barriers between people who need to work together, such as limited or distorted information flows. In addition, there is a need to resolve the fundamental cooperation problem of employees and organizations having different, often conflicting, goals.

Collaboration is an important means to address the challenge of an uncertain environment. Collective knowledge and many diverse minds are better than individuals at dealing with uncertainty. Individuals naturally collaborate. Engage agile techniques to scale collaboration in organizations.

GET WORK DONE

The work environment with culture, purpose, relationships, and collaboration is a competitive advantage when it is free from viruses and enables people to get work done.

Getting work done marks the obvious but not guaranteed in every organization. One should be able to expect a virus free organization. Reality is different.

Does your work environment enable people to get work done?
- Does your culture create glue and a shared mindset?
- Do people find purpose in what they do?
- Do people connect with others to enhance knowledge?
- Do people collaborate across organizational boundaries?

If your answers are no, what can you do?
- Remove the interferences that keep people from getting work done and make the work environment your competitive advantage.

In the following, Chapter 7, we explore competitive advantage Principle #2, Agile.

VIRUS FREE

A virus-free work environment is a competitive advantage as it offers the opportunity for people to get work done. Such a work environment comes with a shared, vibrant culture, clarity of purpose, connectivity through relationships, and collaboration at its core without interference.

KEY CHAPTER IDEAS

- The work environment determines how work gets done.
- Culture creates glue and a shared mindset.
- Purpose drives motivation.
- Relationships connect people to enhance their knowledge.
- Collaboration is needed, as most work involves more than one individual.

ACTION AGENDA

- Evaluate your work environment based on principle #1 Virus Free.
- Follow *Better Management* to make your people get work done and a competitive advantage.

FURTHER READING

Michel, L (2013). *The Performance Triangle: Diagnostic Mentoring to Manage Organizations and People for Superior Performance in Turbulent Times.* London: LID Publishing.

CHAPTER

7

AGILE

Principle #2, Agile, comes with a strategy that clears expectations and results that keep promises and create value.

Does the organization keep its promises and deliver value?

RESULTS

Success is at the top of the triangle (Figure 20) to signal the ultimate goal of an organization: to deliver value and results. Performance, innovation, and growth are key indicators for organizational outcomes. Their balance determines whether the organization enables both exploitation and exploration. The way we set goals and deal with stakeholders determines much of the internal growth capacity of a company.

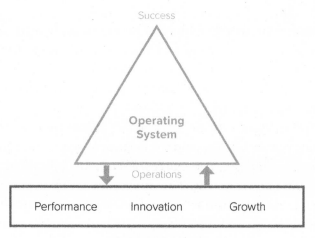

FIGURE 20: RESULTS

Success stands at the top of the Performance Triangle, representing the ultimate goal of management. Successful firms meet or exceed expectations by making performance visible, in the form of socially accepted outcomes.

In the Performance Triangle model, five attributes determine success: responsiveness, the ability to sense opportunities and react to them; alignment of the organization with strategy, a prerequisite to creating value; organizational core competencies, the foundation for sustainable competitive advantage; motivation of the team to get things done; and the wisdom of how the organization defines and uses its boundaries.

The five attributes define the primary, intangible, value-creating elements of an organization, which drive success:

1. **Responsiveness**, to know with clarity. The promise to clients.
2. **Alignment**, to move in one direction. The attractiveness of the strategy.
3. **Capabilities**, to mobilize the energy. The core capabilities and competitive advantage.
4. **Motivation**, to maintain the focus. The aspirations of the entire team.
5. **Cleverness**, to remain in focus. The boundaries of entrepreneurship.

Performance assesses the ability of people to apply their skills and knowledge, access resources and release their full potential with peak performance in mind. The performance metric offers an early indication of the amount of interference that keeps people from exploiting their potential.

The interpretation of the performance metric immediately leads to the inner game, learning and the balance of goals. Inadequate performance is a symptom. The sources of root causes always reside with the operating environment. The inner game is the technique that translates knowledge into action and transfers control to the learner. Awareness, choice, and trust help people focus on what counts. The result is flow (Csikszentmihalyi, 1990) – the state in which learning, performance and joy collide to deliver superior results.

Innovation is a measure of the organization's ability to excite clients with new products and services. The innovation metric signals agile and people-centric capabilities. Innovation and agility are strongly correlated. We know that innovative organizations have agile capabilities, and agile capabilities lead to superior innovations. It's the classic chicken-and-egg problem – which came first? What matters is that agile capabilities lead to superior innovation. In an environment where people can unlock their creativity and create new knowledge, innovation is the outcome. The interpretation of the innovation metric starts with people, their ability to apply their creativity and agility, the systems, culture and leadership that enable superior innovation. Innovation is also the choice for an exploration-type business model. Missing innovation may be a choice or a symptom of the lack of an appropriate environment and management model.

Growth marks the organization's ability to develop from within. The growth metric offers early insights into the capacity for renewal and resilience. It indicates the degree to which the organization captures relevant business opportunities and turns them into stakeholder value.

By using purposeful, cooperative, and knowledge-creating strategies, companies can reinvent themselves with new business models while they preserve their core. The way we set goals and how we deal with stakeholders determine much of the internal growth capacity of a company.

The interpretation of the growth metric leads to the work environment where people have to contribute to value creation, the purpose they find in what they do, the ability to collaborate, and connectedness with others within and outside the organization.

CREATE VALUE

Strategy and results are a competitive advantage when the organization delivers on expectations and creates value. Such organizations come with agile capabilities.

Does your organization deliver on its promises and create value? Is your organization successful: responsive, aligned, capable, motivated, clever?
* Are people able to perform and create value?
* Is the organization innovative?
* Does the business grow?

If your answers are no, what can you do?
* Balance performance, innovation, and growth to make value creation your competitive advantage.

In the following, Chapter 8, we explore competitive advantage Principle #3, People-centric.

AGILE

Better Management delivers on its promises and is a competitive advantage by creating value through being successful, performing at the peak, enabling innovation, and growing from within.

KEY CHAPTER IDEAS

- Results determine whether the organization delivers on promises and create value.
- Success measures responsiveness, alignment, capabilities, motivation, and growth.
- Performance measures whether people can apply their talent.
- Innovation measures the creative capacity of the organization.
- Growth measures the internal development capacity.

ACTION AGENDA

- Evaluate your organization based on Principle #2, Agile.
- Follow *Better Management* to make your work environment create value and gain a competitive advantage.

FURTHER READING

Michel, L (2021). *Management Design: Managing People and Organizations in Turbulent Times* (Third ed.). London: LID Publishing.

CHAPTER

8

PEOPLE-CENTRIC

Principle #3, People-centric, comes with four levers that mobilize resources with self-responsible people who make the client offering specific.

Does management mobilize the resources to create unique value?

MANAGEMENT

Management modes (Figure 21) offer four bundles of managerial principles and capabilities. People-centric is the feature of better management. It is specific when it offers the opportunity for knowledge people to be creative and perform.

FIGURE 21: PEOPLE-CENTRIC MANAGEMENT

Four management levers separate traditional from people-centric management. Traditional management corresponds to a context with concentrated knowledge; people-centric management relates to a context where distributed knowledge dominates. Figure 22 lists the levers that determine the management response part of the dominant management mode.

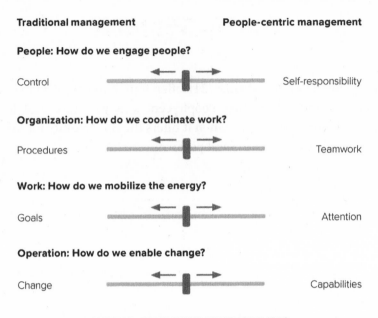

Traditional management   **People-centric management**

People: How do we engage people?

Control   Self-responsibility

Organization: How do we coordinate work?

Procedures   Teamwork

Work: How do we mobilize the energy?

Goals   Attention

Operation: How do we enable change?

Change   Capabilities

FIGURE 22: FOUR MANAGEMENT LEVERS

Each of the above principles warrants an entire book of relevant managerial content. Much has been written about them, and I've explained some of the principles in detail in my other books. I don't want to duplicate that here. It would not do justice to the wealth of insights. Instead, here is my short-version synopsis of what these principles mean:

Control assumes that only managers have the skills and knowledge to know what and how things need to get done. As such, they tell people what to do, and then come and check on whether it has been done.

Self-responsibility assumes that people can think, decide, and act on their own. This allows managers to unlock their creativity, talent, and potential.

Procedures are detailed routines that prescribe how a specific task needs to be performed. This increases predictability, efficiency, and the ability to repeat tasks over and over, with little knowledge requirement.

Teamwork is the approach to getting work done that requires creativity and responsiveness in groups. It's needed when tasks require knowledge and flexibility.

Goals refer to stringent alignment through detailed performance objectives and incentives paid to achieve specific targets. This works well when tasks are simple and context never changes.

Attention is people's ability to focus on the things that truly matter for them and the business. Attention is a limited resource that requires care if it is to deliver full capacity.

Change is the process by which organizations adapt to alterations in the environment through one-time efforts. As change is a sort of replacement for management, it works in a context that is simple and that doesn't change.

Capabilities are the clues to dealing with a dynamic environment where people apply their full talent, creativity, and performance to deal with an ever-changing context.

The principles that emerge from the levers need to align with each other. For example, self-responsibility and detailed goals don't align. They neutralize each other, and, therefore, require resolve.

SPECIFIC

People-centric management is a competitive advantage when it enables people to make the client offering specific.

A specific offering comes with a unique value proposition. People who engage their creativity and dedication make it specific. People-centric management principles mobilize the people's resources.

Is your management people-centric and does it enable people to create a unique value proposition? Does it mobilize people's distinct skills, motivations, and resources?

- Are your levers on the people-centric side?

If your answer is no, what can you do?

- Shift your levers toward people-centric such that people can act on their own as your competitive advantage.

In the following, Chapter 9, we explore competitive advantage Principle #4, In the flow.

PEOPLE-CENTRIC

People-centric management is a competitive advantage, as it mobilizes people and their resources to make the client offering specific. Better Management comes with the choice for people-centric.

KEY CHAPTER IDEAS

- Four levers make people-centric management specific.
- They are self-responsibility, teamwork, attention, and capabilities.
- The choice for people-centric makes management a competitive advantage.

ACTION AGENDA

- Evaluate your management based on Principle #3, People-centric.
- Follow *Better Management* to make your management specific and a competitive advantage.

FURTHER READING

Michel, L (2020). *People-Centric Management: How Managers Use Four Levers to Bring Out the Greatness of Others*. London: LID Publishing.

CHAPTER

9

IN THE FLOW

Principle #4 ensures that people reach flow more often to perform at their peak and exceed expectations. Awareness, choice, trust, and focus of attention are the elements. This makes performance a competitive advantage that is hard to copy.

Can people unfold their potential, learn, and perform at their peak to exceed expectations?

PEOPLE

In *Levers of Control* (2005), Professor Robert Simons of the Harvard Business School states: "To unleash this potential [knowledge workers] managers must overcome organizational blocks. Management control systems play an important role in this process." Over the years, organizational 'viruses' have seeped into many firms, introducing interference in the form of faulty leadership, erroneous systems, or an infected culture, preventing people from performing at their peak.

Performance and creativity require degrees of freedom, self-responsibility and the ability to focus. These are things that are not naturally given in organizations, even though every responsible leader would insist that "everything is under control." Control is the key word for the lack of understanding of what performance is all about. Humanism, propounded by the Enlightenment philosopher Immanuel Kant, introduced the notion of "Humans as the end, not the means." This means that people should not be used to reach higher goals. Creativity, freely interpreted, requires fairness (equality), individualism, and an elevated sense of the purpose of work. Kant calls these the attributes of a modern society.

FIGURE 23: PEOPLE

Four elements (Figure 23) offer insights into the individual environment, with speed as the operation's dynamic capability and performance as the outcome:

- **Focus**, to stay on track
- **Awareness**, to understand and know with clarity
- **Trust**, to act and mobilize the energy
- **Choice**, to move in one direction

Translated into the reality of today's organizations, this means that responsible employees require choice, trust, and purpose to perform. The enabling mode assumes that people are self-motivated and want to get things done fast. This calls for providing them with observation points to focus their attention. Greater awareness means they sense early signs and have a significant degree of freedom to react to them. Choice is the foundation for responsibility. Once people have made their choices, they will need to be trusted to maintain the right focus. The inner-game techniques translate knowledge into action and require an enabling working environment.

Awareness, choice, and trust help people focus their attention on what counts. The result is flow – the state in which learning, performance, and creativity are at their peak (Csikszentmihalyi, 1990). It shifts control to the learner and redefines the role of the leader as a coach.

THE INNER GAME

Executives play the inner game to cope with the challenges of the outer game. They make decisions: understand, think, act, engage and adhere. They accept responsibility and are accountable for their results. They source their motivation from a combination of individual responsibility and the opportunities and systems offered by the institution. Awareness, choice, trust, and focus of attention constitute the inner game.

Awareness involves learning by translating observed data into information without making a judgment about it. It is about having a clear understanding of the present. Nonjudgmental awareness is the best way to learn. Leaders have a choice between self-confident awareness and disengagement through outside control.

Choice is the prerequisite for responsibility. It is the choice to take charge and move in the desired direction. Choice means self-determination, whereas rules are determined from the outside. Leaders need to choose between choice and rules.

Trust means speed and agility. It is the cheapest leadership concept ever invented and the foundation for every business transaction. With trust, there is no need for any renegotiation of contracts when things change. Leaders have the choice between trust and mistrust or responsibility and outside control. But trust must be earned. The best way to earn trust is by delivering on promises.

Focus means self-initiated attention to what matters most. It is a conscious act of concentration that requires energy. The challenge for people is to maintain focus over a period of time. Leaders have the choice between self-initiated focus and goal achievement.

Better Management relies on the executive's ability to play the inner game. The inner game offers the most important principles and techniques for any individual to learn and perform.

HARD TO COPY

People performance is a competitive advantage when it hard to copy.

The inner game offers awareness, choice, trust, and focus as the elements that enable people to unfold their potential and perform beyond expectations. It comes with the flow experience that is hard to copy.

Hard to copy is a competitive advantage as competitors require time, effort, and a considerable investment into people to build these capabilities.

Does management enable people to play the inner game, e.g., fully unfold their potential, learn, and perform at their peak? Are people in the flow? Does it make performance hard to be copied?

- Are awareness, choice, trust, and focus part of your management?

If your answer is no, what can you do?

- Enable people to play the inner game, apply their potential, expedite the learning, and perform as your competitive advantage.

In the following, Chapter 10, we explore competitive advantage Principle #5, Dynamic.

IN THE FLOW

The inner game makes people, their performance, and their ability to quickly learn a competitive advantage as it is hard to copy. Better Management enables people to exceed expectations and reach flow more often.

KEY CHAPTER IDEAS

- The inner game enables flow – the state where people perform at their peak which makes management hard to copy.
- Awareness, choice, trust, and focus of attention are the elements of the inner game.

ACTION AGENDA

- Evaluate your management based on Principle #4, In the flow.
- Follow *Better Management* to make your management hard to copy and a competitive advantage.

FURTHER READING

Michel, L (2021). *Agile by Choice: How You Can Make the Shift to Establish Leadership Everywhere*. London: LID Publishing.

CHAPTER
10

DYNAMIC

Principle #5, Dynamic, means being ready for VUCA with a dynamic operating system that enables people to master higher challenges while, at the same time, it prevents people from taking shortcuts.

Does the operating system enable the organization to master higher challenges? Does it prevent shortcuts?

OPERATING SYSTEM

Management modes (Figure 24) offer bundles of managerial principles and capabilities. Dynamic is a feature of Better Management. It enables the organization do deal with a VUCA context and limits the risks by preventing people from taking shortcuts. Shortcuts undermine the operating system and create an infected culture.

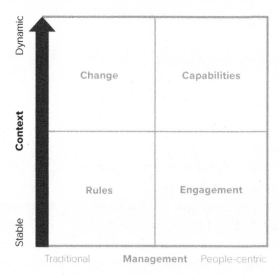

FIGURE 24: DYNAMIC CONTEXT

Similar to the people-centric levers, four context levers add more depth to the analysis and separate a stable context from a dynamic one. Traditional tools, routines, interactions, and standards work well in a stable management context. However, they fail to support management in a dynamic context. For a dynamic context, the entire toolbox requires a design with dynamic features. Figure 25 lists the levers that determine the context part of the dominant management mode.

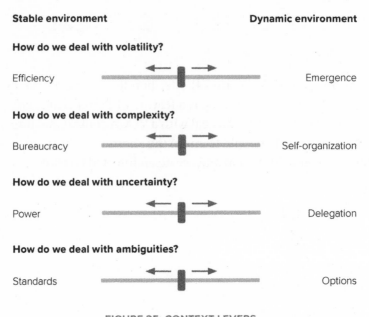

Stable environment   **Dynamic environment**

How do we deal with volatility?

Efficiency   Emergence

How do we deal with complexity?

Bureaucracy   Self-organization

How do we deal with uncertainty?

Power   Delegation

How do we deal with ambiguities?

Standards   Options

FIGURE 25: CONTEXT LEVERS

Context levers offer options that vary depending on whether the environment is stable or dynamic:

Efficiency is the hallmark of traditional management. While no business succeeds without it, a pure focus on cost, productivity, and risk prevention leaves no room for creativity and emergence. Efficiency with tight performance objectives hooks businesses into operating with the use of tools designed for a stable environment.

Emergence means flexibility and anticipation. The tools focus attention on the things that matter and trust in developing the capabilities that can handle a dynamic context.

Bureaucracy involves rigorous processes that work well in a stable context. But they are not flexible enough to deal with complexity. While routines provide a stable platform, they need the dynamic design to support complexity.

Self-organization relies on teams with flexible routines to deal with increasing complexity. Teams with delegated authority outperform managers in a dynamic context.

Power works in a stable environment where outcomes are easily determined. Power relies on managers who know what they're doing and act accordingly.

Delegation and trust are the clues to managing in an uncertain context. In times of uncertainty, trust in oneself and one's own capabilities are helpful in dealing with it. Leaders who delegate and offer trust deserve respect.

Standards as 'standard operating procedure' work well in a stable and clear context. When outcomes can be predetermined, standards work well.

Options are needed in a time of ambiguous contexts. Using mental models that can deal with multiple outcomes can help you succeed in a dynamic environment.

The dominant principles that emerge from the levers need to align with each other. For example, emergence and centralized power for decisions don't align – they contradict each other.

NO SHORTCUTS

A dynamic operating system is a competitive advantage when it prevents people from taking shortcuts.

Managers and employees who take shortcuts around the prevailing operating system, e.g. detour routines and rules to get to the destination faster, undermine the culture. If it is okay not to follow given standards and policies, then this results in a culture where everything is fine – just don't get caught.

Organizations can prevent shortcuts with an operating system that commits everyone to using it because it helps getting things done better and faster. Such an operating system sets the standard and the policy that leads to a culture where everyone trusts the system and follows it.

An operating system that can handle a dynamic environment has the features that prevents people from taking shortcuts. It leads to a trusted culture where there is no need to get around the system.

Is your operating system ready for a volatile, uncertain, complex, and ambiguous environment? Does it enable people to master higher challenges without taking shortcuts?

- Are your levers on the dynamic side?

If your answer is no, what can you do?

- Develop your operating system such that it shifts your context levers to dynamic and turns itself into a competitive advantage.

In the following Chapter 11, we explore competitive advantage Principle #6, Interactive and diagnostic.

DYNAMIC

The choice for a dynamic operating system is a competitive advantage, as it enables people to master higher challenges without shortcuts. Better Management enables people to deal with disruptions, uncertainty, volatility, ambiguity, and complexity.

KEY CHAPTER IDEAS

- Four levers make the operating system dynamic and prevent shortcuts.
- They are emergence, self-organization, delegation, and options.
- The choice for dynamic makes management a competitive advantage.

ACTION AGENDA

- Evaluate your management based on Principle #5, Dynamic.
- Follow *Better Management* to make your management prevent shortcuts and a competitive advantage.

FURTHER READING

Michel, L (2021). *Management Design: Managing People and Organizations in Turbulent Times* (Third ed.). London: LID Publishing.

CHAPTER

11

INTERACTIVE
AND DIAGNOSTIC

Principle #6, Interactive and diagnostic, comes with a toolbox that is deeply embedded in the culture of the organization. It enables interaction and diagnostic control in ways that support people to capture new opportunities and grow.

Does your toolbox enable the organization to capture new opportunities as they arise? Is it deeply embedded in culture?

THE TOOLBOX

Leadership and systems (Figure 26) combine the elements of the toolbox. Leadership needs to interact and facilitate the conversation around purpose, direction, and performance. Systems that work diagnostically direct attention to the issues that matter most to the business and allow people to act in a self-organized and decentralized manner.

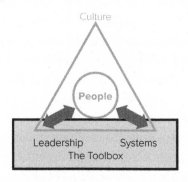

FIGURE 26: THE TOOLBOX

There are two ways to influence what people do:

1. Leaders can directly influence people through interaction and interference. They can tell them what to do and how to do it. Leadership interaction is heavy work. It requires energy and time.

2. Systems – governing strategy, mission, objectives and the like – direct and influence people. Systems work like autopilot. Once set, they serve their purpose and influence people.

Both ways of influencing human behaviour need to be in balance. Interactive leadership and dynamic systems make organizations agile. They help people detect weak market signals early from feedback data, allow for the interpretation of that information, and facilitate timely action to address it. These are the features of an agile organization and the foundation for innovation.

Both elements offer insights in the toolbox. These elements include:

- **Leadership**, the sense-making, strategy, performance, contribution, and risk conversations.
- **Systems**, the information, strategy, implementation, beliefs and boundary rules, routines and tools.

Interactive leadership is about the personal interaction between leaders and employees. Dynamic systems offer the rules, routines, and tools to get work done. Leadership and systems are a competitive advantage when they are deeply rooted in culture.

Leadership is a key component of the triangle. In today's organizations, be they a small group in a traditional structure, a community or an ecosystem, leadership is exercised wherever it influences other people's thinking, behaviours, decisions, and actions. Leadership is not necessarily tied to traditional positions with power in hierarchies.

Effective leaders in agile organizations interact with people on a personal level, relate to others to facilitate meaningful collaboration, and establish a supportive work environment based on a culture of trust. In the broadest sense, leadership is communication and interaction with others at all levels, vertically and horizontally, throughout an organization. We suggest that leaders in any organization develop effective communication and interaction skills that are natural and unique to them.

The traditional notion is that the culture of an organization is shaped at the top of the management hierarchy and cascades downward. We generally accept this belief. However, in many organizations we've seen a huge disconnect between what top executives think is going on and what the rank-and-file employees actually believe.

Leaders and managers at all levels must recognize that their actions and behaviours are being observed and interpreted by employees through the lens of their own beliefs and values. Many leaders, perhaps inadvertently, fail to connect with employees, and they communicate conflicting values and beliefs throughout the organization. Employees will rarely approach the CEO and say, "You said this, but we actually did that. Which is it, and what's going on?" The result is that employees are left to develop their own interpretations, which is, in many cases, inconsistent with organizational goals.

Leading requires fluency in things that are probably unnatural for most of us. Teaming and interaction mean that leaders take interpersonal risks. True teaming requires a sense of psychological safety and stepping back to see others' perspectives. It's about losing traditional control to gain real control.

Leadership is a complex and indefinable quality, but we've identified five unconscious (and rarely discussed) attributes that contribute to strengthening the culture and performance of the organization.

Five conversations can be had as interactions to exercise leadership control. They are as follows:

1. **Sense-making** discussion, to understand and know with clarity.
2. **Strategy conversation**, to think and move in one direction.
3. **Performance conversation**, to act and mobilize the energy.
4. **Contribution dialogue**, to engage and maintain the focus.
5. **Risk dialogue**, to adhere to and maintain the focus.

Systems are located at the lower-right corner of the triangle. They represent the institutional toolbox, with rules, routines, and resources that set the stage for rigorous and disciplined leadership. It's about systems support implementation with the right balance of freedom and constraint. Supporting collaboration between people and systems provides the fuel to power the formation of beliefs and decisions. This is essential for identifying purpose. In addition, systems set boundaries to achieve the desired balance between entrepreneurship and efficiency.

Systems are both influenced by and influence the culture and leadership practices that shape the decision-making process. When we talk about systems, we aren't just talking about IT systems, but the rules and routines that shape the input and output from computerized tools. Everyone reading this chapter is familiar with the phrases 'garbage in, garbage out' and 'what gets measured, gets done.' However, we contend that such thinking is just scratching the surface of the complex dimension we call systems. What managers and employees do with the output from IT systems, and how that output shapes decisions and behaviours, is rarely considered. Similarly, we've witnessed many examples of systems developed in prior decades being used to drive decisions today, despite the fact that the business dynamic – and the wider world around us – has changed dramatically. We have seen many instances where managers created systems to generate relevant data needed to solve some problem, or give the organization an edge, 20 years ago. The problem was solved, partially with the aid of the data, and the company gained an edge over competitors.

Today, though, managers are making decisions using information that is no longer relevant because their approach was established decades ago, and the competitive dynamics have changed significantly. What was relevant and meaningful 20 years ago may not be today, leading to regrettable decisions. It therefore becomes imperative for leaders to constantly evaluate whether the old rules, routines, and tools being used to drive decisions are still relevant, and whether they shape desired behaviours.

We have identified five questions, the answers to which provide insight into unconscious and rarely examined beliefs, values, and shared assumptions that either inhibit or enable the effectiveness of systems. The system of work and the system of management are interconnected. Changing the system of work will not yield performance if the operating system that governs it remains flawed.

Five diagnostic systems support people to get work done with the benefit of:

1. **Information** – to understand and know with clarity.
2. **Strategy** – to think and move in one direction.
3. **Implementation** – to act and mobilize the energy.
4. **Beliefs** – to engage and maintain the focus.
5. **Boundaries** – to adhere to and maintain the focus.

DEEPLY EMBEDDED
IN CULTURE

An interactive and diagnostic toolbox is a competitive advantage when it is deeply embedded in culture.

Culture works like glue. When routines and policies are embedded in culture, then leaders can rely on people to use the toolbox as if it is their own. As such, the organization becomes consistent and reliable. And a deeply anchored toolbox reduces cost. These routines and policies become an automatism and can be used over and over in various context. They stick with the organization and make people use them.

Is your toolbox deeply embedded in culture? Is it built to enable people to capture new opportunities?

- Do leaders and systems have a design that supports people to take risks as entrepreneurs and grow?

If your answer is no, what can you do?

- Remove the bureaucracy that keeps people from capturing new opportunities and make leadership and systems your competitive advantage.

In the following, Part III, we will explore the design of Better Management as a competitive advantage.

INTERACTIVE AND DIAGNOSTIC

Better Management comes with a toolbox with leadership and systems that is deeply embedded in culture. As such, it is a competitive advantage that enables people to capture new opportunities.

KEY CHAPTER IDEAS

- Leadership and systems include a toolbox that is rooted in culture.
- Embed entrepreneurship as a key value in your culture.
- The design of the toolbox makes leadership and systems a competitive advantage.

ACTION AGENDA

- Evaluate your toolbox based on Principle #6, Interactive and Diagnostic.
- Follow *Better Management* to make your toolbox part of the culture and a competitive advantage.

FURTHER READING

Michel, L (2021). *Diagnostic Mentoring: How to Transform the Way We Manage*. London: LID Publishing.

PART III

MANAGEMENT DESIGN

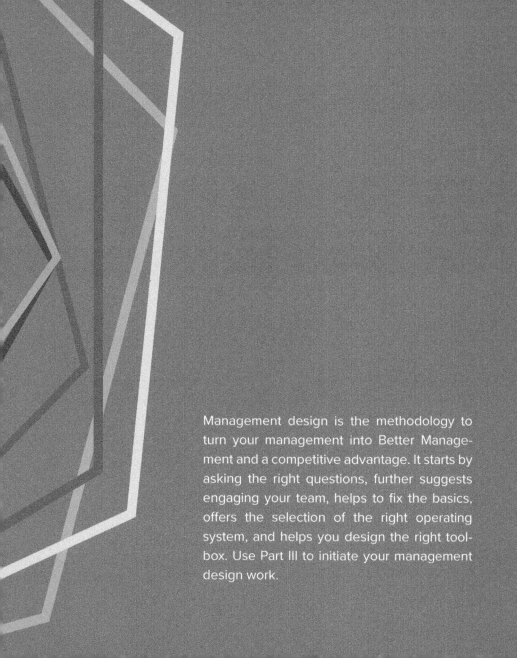

Management design is the methodology to turn your management into Better Management and a competitive advantage. It starts by asking the right questions, further suggests engaging your team, helps to fix the basics, offers the selection of the right operating system, and helps you design the right toolbox. Use Part III to initiate your management design work.

CHAPTER
12

ASK
QUESTIONS

Asking questions creates awareness. The management design framework establishes a shared language that supports people to think about what it takes to turn your management into a competitive advantage. It focuses the conversation on Better Management. The management canvas frames the questions on people, organization, work, operations, and management.

THE MANAGEMENT CANVAS

The canvas tool helps us facilitate conversations and interventions. It captures five dimensions in a template, with questions you can use to document your understanding of the diagnostic results. The five dimensions originate from the Performance Triangle. The four management levers come from *People-Centric Management* (Michel, 2020). As such, the canvas combines the agile and people-centric models with a facilitation tool. Figure 27 shows the alignment of the Performance Triangle model with five frames. Five pairs of questions guide the diagnosis, the sense-making and the learning. Within each pair, the first question is about work on the system, while the second question guides your work in the system. The switch from question one to question two prepares you to transition from your individual journey to one you'll make with your team and the entire organization.

- **People**: How do I engage people?
  How do we know with clarity?
- **Organization**: How do I coordinate work?
  How do we move in one direction?
- **Work**: How do I mobilize the energy?
  How do we mobilize resources?
- **Operations**: How do I enable development?
  How do we maintain the focus?
- **Management**: How do I manage the organization?
  How do we lead in the people-centric way?

The canvas comprises your notes for your agile journey. Use it as follows:
- **Assumptions**, principles, and potential (green Post-it notes) and sources of interference (red Post-its): the diagnostic offers the relevant observation points.
- **Gaps** (yellow Post-its): the difference between your current situation and your desired situation reflects the gaps that require your attention.

- **Key issues** (dark blue Post-its): the themes you've decided to work on spotlight your focus areas.
- **Initiatives** (grey Post-its): these translate key issues into initiatives that help you address the gaps.
- **Road map** (bright blue Post-its): this weaves schedules and resources initiatives into a programme that will ensure that your organization makes the transition to better management.

The canvas is a template that can be used as a poster, for a team to work with in a workshop setting. The use of coloured Post-it notes helps separate the above steps.

Every frame represents a distinct choice of concepts:

People: Organizations comprise people who apply their knowledge, experience, and skills to perform and deliver value. They want to apply their creativity and full potential. The way in which we engage people determines much of the speed of an organization.

Organization: Culture, leadership and systems frame the operating environment that enable people to apply their creativity, seize opportunities, and stimulate innovation. The way in which we organize collaboration determines so much of the agility of an organization.

Work: In most cases, modern work requires more than one person. It involves multiple stakeholders. People who work have needs, expectations and offer resources to an organization. The challenge is to enable collaboration, stimulate relationships, and provide purpose for growth. The way in which we set goals determines much of the resilience of an organization.

Operations: Operations help people cope with internal and external challenges. The environment poses a variety of challenges to people, organization, management, and operations. Creativity, innovation, and growth determine the overall performance of an organization. The way in which we deal with change determines much of the scope of management's ability to act.

Management: Every manager's task is to create an environment in which people make entrepreneurial decisions to provide superior value to clients. The way in which we make decisions determines much of how we get things done – our actions.

Asking questions raises the awareness for Better Management.

Are you clear about Better Management for your organization?

- Have you answered the questions?

If your answer is no, what can you do?

- Use Appendix 1 Map your challenges to initiate your questioning.

In the following, Chapter 13, we recommend that you answer these questions with your team.

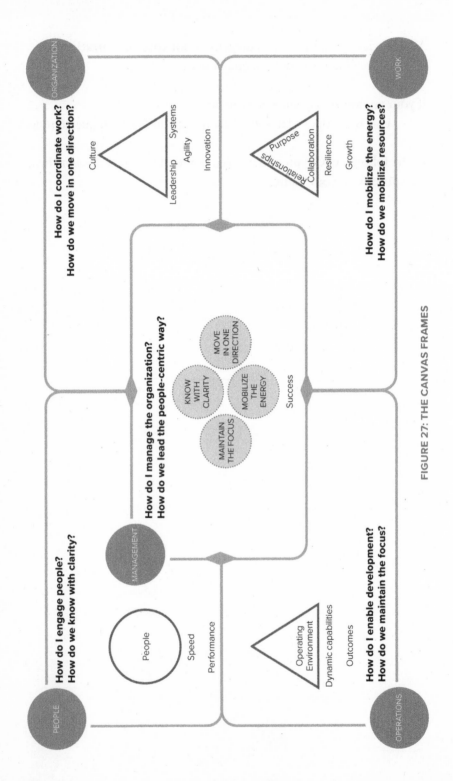

FIGURE 27: THE CANVAS FRAMES

ASK QUESTIONS

The management design framework offers five frames with questions that initiate the design for Better Management.

KEY CHAPTER IDEAS

- People, organization, work, operations, and management are the frames for a conversation about Better Management.

ACTION AGENDA

- Ask questions.
- Capture your answers with the canvas poster.

FURTHER READING

Michel, L (2021). *Management Design: Managing People and Organizations in Turbulent Times* (Third ed.). London: LID Publishing.

CHAPTER

13

ENGAGE
THE TEAM

Diagnostic mentoring is the three-step methodology to develop Better Management. Engage your team to collectively raise awareness, act on insights, learn fast, and turn your management into a competitive advantage.

DIAGNOSTIC MENTORING

The journey to Better Management is a transformation where no one has the answers on the specific tools and practices that make up people-centric management, an agile organization, and a dynamic operating system. It's a process that requires individual design, to fit it to the specific needs of the organization and its stakeholders. As such, the shift to better management is a transformation that follows design-thinking in three steps: collectively raise awareness, act on insights, and learn fast.

1. **Raise awareness**.
   Diagnose current capabilities, create awareness.
2. **Act on insights**.
   Identify the desired capability insights for decisions.
3. **Learn fast**.
   Enable better, people-centric management through agile capabilities and dynamic systems.

If you look at steps as part of a stairway, you can walk up and down these stairs. If you look at steps as a sequence of stages or things, you can go forward but also backward. You can take a step back. The three-step transformation works like that. It's not a prescription for a start, and then one step, then two, then three, and you're finished. The three steps represent three mandatory parts that logically follow each other. But, more often than not, one goes back to 'step one' for a fresh look. The steps are circular in how they're applied.

Mentoring applies the inner game to design. The self-mentoring process is central to the principles outlined in my book, *Agile by Choice*. It is the same approach that my organization's agile experts use when they work with their executive clients. As such, mentoring follows the same principles that establish the foundation of agile leadership, organization and management: awareness, insights and learning.

The three steps combine individual, team, and organizational perspectives into a coherent approach. This establishes an institutional framework for a reflective opening of perspectives through authentic dissent as a tool to learn about people-centric, agile, and dynamic capabilities. The exchange and dissent on observations is what creates new insights and knowledge. Interaction and discourse are based on common language that establishes a shared language.

Figure 28 looks at capabilities that can be observed, modelled, and transformed. In a systems view, monitoring and 'dynamization' can be treated as two separate functions (Luhmann, 1995). The science of cybernetics calls this second-order observing systems (von Foerster, 1992). The way we do things becomes a subject of reflection and is opened up to alternatives. Through observation, capabilities become revisable.

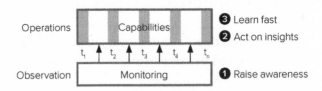

FIGURE 28: DIAGNOSTIC MENTORING

Raise awareness: The diagnostic establishes observation points. Monitoring is a discipline that can be used to observe and alter design. By observing (scanning) capabilities, potential faults and malfunctions can be spotted at an early stage. By becoming aware of critical signals, potential design requirements can be identified. In this way, leaders can decide whether or not to address certain issues. As such, monitoring initiates design changes relating to capabilities.

Diagnostics are the sensing tools that help you see the invisible: your potential, and the interference that keeps you from delivering your expected outcomes. Observation points help you identify the systemic relationships between the critical elements of your organization, to help distil your dominant assumptions, principles, and patterns. Awareness turns opinions into meaning, to create purpose.

Act on insights: The Performance Triangle (see Chapter 2) distils the elements of agile. The use of agile capabilities and design is selective. The decision to employ a specific design excludes other alternatives. The design process is about the selection of managerial tools, routines, and rules that make organizations agile. Design requires reflection and interactions. It is not free from politics. The setting of these conversations determines much about the design's quality.

The five dimensions – people, organization, work, operations, and management – create a shared language for the transformation. With the help of diagnostic mentors, you can identify the critical intervention points and articulate your ideal design, with gaps and key issues. Your design choices will take you from symptoms to root causes, with clarity on where to interfere.

Learn fast: The inner game (see Chapter 9) offers the techniques involved in following the agile way of learning. Monitoring assumes that the design is reversible, not frozen in place. While deeply embedded in organizational practices and rooted in the past, managerial design, and capabilities can be changed through interventions. The people-centric shift guides specific capability development projects in line with decisions on what needs to be changed. In this way, the idea of permanent change is replaced by the notion of combining learning and doing. It is an iterative process.

Expertise will help you transform your management and organization and develop people-centric, agile and dynamic capabilities at scale. Trust yourself to identify the initiatives that will offer the most leverage on how to switch from idea to action. Establish a road map for how you and your team can collaborate, using your management skills to create superior value.

The three-step diagnostic mentoring process is how executives develop better management with their teams.

- ` Have you engaged your team in the process?

If your answer is no, what can you do?

- Consider making diagnostic mentoring a team approach.

With the following, Chapter 14, first fix the basics, then develop fitness.

ENGAGE THE TEAM

Three-step diagnostic mentoring is the methodology to develop better management. It applies the inner game techniques to raise awareness, act on insights, and learn fast.

KEY CHAPTER IDEAS

- Diagnostics help to raise awareness.
- Insights from the diagnostic offer choices to close the gaps.
- Learning fast is about translating knowledge to action.

ACTION AGENDA

- Apply diagnostic mentoring.
- Engage your team.

FURTHER READING

Michel, L (2021). *Diagnostic Mentoring: How to Transform the Way We Manage*. London: LID Publishing.

CHAPTER
14

FIRST FIX THE BASICS ...

Over time, viruses infect the organization and spread themselves, unwillingly and unknowingly. The task is to first fix the basics, then set the standards to establish fitness. Start now by identifying the current gaps and key issues to close the gaps.

ELIMINATE
INTERFERENCE

In his legendary management book, *Levers of Control* (1995), Harvard Business Professor Robert Simons states: "To unleash this potential [knowledge people], managers must overcome organizational blocks. Management control systems play an important role in this process." Over the years, organizational 'viruses' have invaded many firms unintentionally and unwillingly, interfering in the form of faulty leadership, erroneous systems or an infected culture, preventing people performing at their peak.

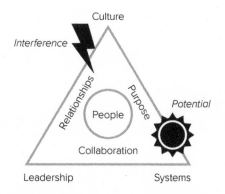

FIGURE 29: POTENTIAL AND INTERFERENCE

Such organizations are ill-prepared for both future challenges and knowledge work and, at the same time, interferences keep them from using their full potential. As a result, organizations are slow in implementation, inflexible and unable to change, too fragile to withstand external shocks, and often unable to act. The symptoms are operating failures, lack of quality of services, misbehaviours, a lack of loyalty, a distorted brand and, eventually, negative public attention driving the downward spiral.

In most cases, it is not 'incompetent management' that causes these issues. Simply put, their management has a design rooted in the industrial age, effective only in a stable environment, and management tools that have lost their impact or fallen by the wayside altogether in today's fast-moving environment. There are two ways to fix the problem: first, to increase the potential or, second, to remove the interferences. As most interferences stem from faulty systems, it is obvious that you should fix the operating system of an organization before investing in the potential of people.

The initial step is to identify the 'viruses' and pinpoint how they limit the potential of the organization and the talent (Figure 29).

SET THE STANDARDS

Better Management follows a distinct set of standards. Foundations, elements and principles distinguish traditional and better management (Figure 30). The task is to commit to the set of standards before interfering into the workings of the organization.

	Traditional Management	Better Management
Foundations		
Goal	Extract value	Create value
Context	Stable context	Dynamic context
Core process	Operational excellence	Balancing efficiency and innovation
Elements		
Culture	Pay per performance	Shared values and norms
Leadership	Control and command	Individualized interaction
Systems	Standardization	Dynamic support and scaling
Purpose	Paid to do work	Apply knowledge and skills
Collaboration	Competition	Natural cooperation
Relationships	Hierarchy	Source of new knowledge
Principles		
Operations	Control	Enabling
Management	Traditional	People-centric
Organization	Traditional	Agile
Toolbox	Traditional	Dynamic

FIGURE 30: SET STANDARDS

The foremost goal of Better Management is to create value for its stakeholders. Management operates in a dynamic context. Most strategies require a balance of efficiency and innovation.

Culture works like glue. For Better Management, it offers shared values and norms. Leadership caters to the individual to ensure ongoing interaction: meeting in person rather than just writing emails. Systems have a design that enables people to perform and respond to greater challenges. They facilitate the scaling of operations. People find purpose and are motivated to apply their knowledge and skills. Collaboration happens naturally in small teams. Networks and relationships are a source of knowledge.

The operating system's primary function is to enable people to get work done and perform. Management follows people-centric principles, and the organization is agile in how it responds to challenges as they arise. The toolbox has a design to enable the organization to operate in a dynamic context.

DEVELOP
FITNESS

The previous chapter, Engage The Team, now serves as the foundation to evaluate the fitness of your management. Management fitness is handy, as it allows managers to compare the capabilities of their organization with others in the same category. And the fitness measurement tool helps managers spot areas that need attention on one page (Figure 31).

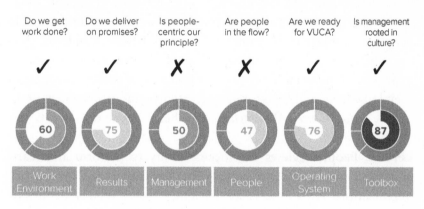

FIGURE 31: SIX LEVELS OF FITNESS

Six levels of fitness offer an actionable overview, with the option to dig deeper. Every level comes with a specific standard that we have identified: a tick means that the organization fulfils the criteria; a cross signals work ahead.

Level 1: Work Environment reviews the capabilities that make up an engaging work environment. The threshold signifies 'solid organizational practices 101,' related to culture, purpose, relationships, and collaboration. Can people fully engage and perform? To reach Level 1 standards, remove the interference that keeps people from engaging in the digital economy.

Use *The Performance Triangle* (Michel, 2013) to dig deeper.

Level 2: Results reviews the elements that represent outcomes. The threshold is an average organization that delivers in the green zone on people performance, innovation, growth, and success factors. Does the organization deliver results? To reach Level 2 standards, determine the elements of your results and identify the levers that will help you build the desired capabilities.

Use *Agile by Choice* (Michel, 2021) to dig deeper.

Level 3: Management reviews the principles of management, with traditional or people-centric capabilities. The threshold is a score of 75, which indicates strong people-centric principles. People-centric principles build self-responsibility and promote delegated decision-making among knowledge workers. Does management enable people to mobilize their resources? To reach Level 3 standards, shift the focus of your management to people-centric principles and a management model that unlocks the potential of people and engages their knowledge and skills for more creativity, innovation and growth.

Use *People-Centric Management* (Michel, 2020) to dig deeper.

Level 4: People reviews employees' ability to perform and learn based on inner-game principles. The standard is set by top-tier organizations with a score of 75. High scores enable people to experience flow more often. Can people unlock their potential and performance at the peak? To reach Level 4 standards, identify the principles of the inner game to focus your attention and release more energy in times of stress. Learn how to deal with adversity and master unexpected challenges.

Use *Agile by Choice* (Michel, 2021) to dig deeper.

Level 5: Operating System reviews the range of capabilities between traditional and dynamic. The standard is set at 75 for dynamic capabilities. Dynamic capabilities enable organizations to better deal with internal and external challenges. Can operations deal with disruptions, volatility, and complexity? To reach Level 5 standards, align the systems principles with your challenges and equip your operating system with dynamic features.

Use *Management Design* (Michel, 2017, 2nd ed.) to dig deeper.

Level 6: Toolbox reviews the fit with people. The standard is set by organizations in the top tier and a score of 75. High scores indicate a toolbox that enables people to deliver peak performance and take on greater challenges. Does the toolbox support people in tackling tougher new challenges? To reach Level 6 standards, design your toolbox with interactive and diagnostic features that perfectly fit your principles, the challenges, and the demographics of your organization.

Use *Diagnostic Mentoring* (Michel, 2021) to dig deeper.

In the example in Figure 31, management passes the first two levels, work environment and results. However, it misses management and people. Both levels are related, as they deal with the people side in organizations. The organization achieves both systems levels, the operating system, and the toolbox.

The six levels of fitness offer a first-cut review of capabilities. The levels show increasing sophistication, with Level 1 being the easiest and Level 6 the most difficult to achieve. As with the example in Figure 31, it is possible to reach higher levels without passing lower levels, as they are all independent. Fixing missing levels starts with the low-hanging fruit; the easier levels only then align with the more challenging levels. In the example, the first fix would be management, then people.

Now, it is up to you to turn to the management design framework and the canvas template to answer the following questions with your team:

What are the gaps? What are the key issues?

People: What is my talents' ability to apply its creativity? How do we enable the inner game for superior speed?

Organization: What is my organization's ability to innovate? How do we establish a work environment for superior agility?

Work: What is my organization's ability to grow? How do we create the connectivity for superior resilience?

Operations: What is my organization's ability to perform? How do we develop the capabilities for a superior ability to act?

Management: What is my management's ability to unlock the organization's potential? How do we build the tools for Better Management?

Start with fixing the basics then engage in diagnostic mentoring to develop fitness.

- Have you engaged in developing fitness in management?

If your answer is no, what can you do?

- Distil the gaps and key issues with your team.
- Consider diagnostic mentoring as your approach.

With the following, Chapter 15, decide on your dominant operating system.

FIRST FIX THE BASICS

Fixing 'infected' elements of the Performance Triangle has first priority. Then, set the standards and start developing fitness in Better Management.

KEY CHAPTER IDEAS

- Fix the basics by limiting interference from 'viruses.'
- Standards distinguish traditional from Better Management.
- Six levels indicate the fitness for Better Management.

ACTION AGENDA

- Eliminate interference with the Performance Triangle elements.
- Set the standards for Better Management.
- Follow the six levels to develop fitness.

FURTHER READING

Michel, L (2021). *Diagnostic Mentoring: How to Transform the Way We Manage*. London: LID Publishing.

CHAPTER
15

SELECT YOUR OPERATING SYSTEM

In line with the dominant operating mode, Better Management requires a dedicated operating system. The choices include four generic rules-based, change-based, engagement-based, and capabilities-based operating systems with entirely different features. More than not, hybrid modes and dual operating systems are needed to balance exploitation and exploration.

FOUR OPERATING SYSTEMS

Better Management requires an operating system that fits the needs of people and the context, and comes with people-centric, agile, and dynamic features. Before we dig into the details of design, it is time to distinguish four dominant operating systems. While they never exist in pure form, they offer guidance for those on the way to deciding on their operating system.

Domestication is a distinctive feature of operating systems and, at the same time, a barrier to changing operating systems. Domestication translates explicit systems into implicit values, capabilities, and behaviours that are deeply embedded in culture. Culture works like glue. This makes it hard to reconfigure operating systems.

It won't come as a surprise that managers and employees are expected to make quick decisions, focus their actions on what matters most, and demonstrate entrepreneurial behaviours in everything they do.

Reality strikes and offers something even more startling. In the context of our information-rich, dynamic environment, the requirements and expectations outlined above are virtually impossible to meet – people are distracted, struggle with decisions, and miss opportunities. As such, managers and employees often have no choice but to act in a self-interested manner. As a consequence, talent is not effectively used and companies perform far below their potential. This challenge is endemic in the dynamic and knowledge-driven environment in which we have become comfortably uncomfortable.

Systematic information overload, analysis paralysis, endless meetings, bias toward rationality, risk-aversity, and blindly following rules dominate our ways of thinking and doing at work. This comes at the expense of disciplined decision-making, deliberate actions and behaviours aligned with company beliefs and boundaries. We know that this is the result of strong domestication.

In a virus-infected culture, faulty leadership and erroneous managerial systems lead to flawed decisions, missing action and undesired behaviours. The negative domestication spiral accelerates because of this deteriorating operating environment. Domestication is what we define as the behaviours and actions of leaders and employees that follow the habits and patterns determined by the organization's rules, norms, and values.

On the positive side, a vibrant culture, interactive leadership, and supportive systems enable fast decisions, actions with impact, and the desired behaviours. These are the outcomes of an operating system with a deliberate design, leading to positively domesticated behaviours; these companies enable a high degree of individual effectiveness where the talent is effectively used.

People follow given rules. They want to do well. That's why the operating system is so important. It domesticates how people decide, act and behave. It is deeply embedded in the organization's culture. With this comes the challenge of responding when the operating system requires change. Changing operating systems influences the rules, routines, and tools people follow. Taking all of that into account, how can organizations jump-start positive domestication?

The idea of positive socialization starts with every individual's return on management (ROM). Harvard Business School Professor Robert Simons developed the concept in 1995, based on the fact that time, attention, and energy are scarce resources for anyone. To achieve a high ROM, it's wise to carefully invest time and focus attention to generate a maximum amount of productive energy. We know that many leaders and employees struggle with this.

ROM = Productive energy released/time and attention invested

An operating system must yield a high ROM (Figure 32). It supports individual effectiveness, time, attention, energy, and organizational effectiveness through efficiency, innovation, and value creation.

Effectiveness	Exploitation	Exploration	Outcome
Individual	Time	Attention	Energy
Organizational	Efficiency	Innovation	Value creation

FIGURE 32: RETURN ON MANAGEMENT

Figure 33 positions four operating systems in line with the operating modes: rules, engagement, change, and enabling. Each has a different purpose and outcome that spans traditional and people-centric.

Managers can choose and mix four operating systems, depending on the specific managerial context in which their organizations operate.

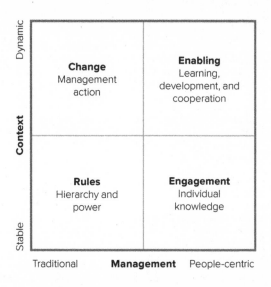

FIGURE 33: FOUR OPERATING SYSTEMS

The rapidly changing environment and a tech-savvy generation's knowledge and talents force companies to be clear about the operating mode.

Four questions help us distinguish the four operating modes:

1. How do we engage people and know with clarity?
2. How do we make superior decisions and move in one direction?
3. How do we coordinate work and mobilize the energy?
4. How do we enable performance and maintain the focus?

Capabilities-based operating systems call for self-responsible, collective decisions, with a focus on learning and development. In rules-based operating systems, decisions are deferred to senior management, at the top of the hierarchy. Engagement-based systems facilitate collective debate and motivation, whereas, with change-based systems, management takes corrective action. Figure 34 summarizes the features of the four generic operating systems.

Operation	Rules	Change	Engagement	Enabling
Culture, leadership, and system	Hierarchy and power	Management action	Individual knowledge	Learning and development
Context	Comparably stable environment	High uncertainty and pace	Knowledge- and technology-intensive	High complexity and ambiguity
How we understand and engage	Leaders motivate, extrinsic rewards	Stretched goals and incentives	Mastery and meaning	Self-responsibility and purpose
How we think and decide	Through hierarchy	By leaders	Debate and reason	Collective wisdom
How we act and coordinate	Processes and operating procedures	Change projects	Projects, workshops, and meetings	Self-organization, mutual adjustment
How we behave and motivate	Top-down goals and control	Aligned action	Self-interest	Wide goals, shared mindset

FIGURE 34: FEATURES OF OPERATING SYSTEMS

Operating systems come with a toolbox for leaders and employees that helps them use time effectively, focus attention, and mobilize the productive energy.

The dominant operating system varies, depending on the business context in which a company operates. More often than not, companies unwillingly or unknowingly operate with mixed (or multiple) operating systems that vary within the organization. My research confirms that 45% of companies still operate in the rules-based operating mode.

For example, a global pharmaceutical company I worked with used the engagement mode for its research and development function, while its manufacturing part applied the control-based system.

The selection and design of the toolbox for each mode of operations is a senior executive task that requires experience.

In a highly regulated, safety-first context, the rules-based operating systems may still be effective. Change-based operating systems are the norm in transaction-oriented and heavily technology-supported industries, such as insurance, banking, and telecom. Engagement-based operating systems do well in knowledge-driven environments, such as educational institutions or professional services businesses.

Counterintuitively, operating systems can be observed in a variety of settings that require both a high degree of flexibility and a rigorous set of operating procedures. This is certainly the case in the work of a commercial airline pilot, the emergency room of a hospital, a military unit in a combat situation, or a firefighting company. These examples do not illustrate normal, everyday business operations, but looking at the extremes helps to make the point.

Nobody would ever go into a restaurant kitchen and ask for the specifics of a recipe before ordering a meal. It is expected that the chef knows what he's doing.

In an emergency room, we trust the exceptional skills of highly trained doctors, nurses, and technicians who intuitively do what is right in that specific situation and context. They're trained to follow strict standards, but when the situation requires, it is their skills rather than the routines that save lives. Agility and capabilities beat rigorous routines.

In military combat or a firefighting situation, leaders can only provide broad guidance on how to go about handling a specific emergency. On the battlefield or at the scene of a fire, well-developed skills and intuition are required to do what is necessary. No command from above could ever be better at reacting quickly and flexibly to fit the situation. Soldiers and firefighters respond in the best way their intuition and trained behaviours allow. They've absorbed rigorous procedures on how to deal with emergencies and can simultaneously exhibit flexibility and resilience.

Well-developed operating systems facilitate intuitive decision-making (the agile elements) and trained routine (the stable elements) rather than authority, blind action, and decision-by-paralysis. And so, they allow for fast responses, permit flexible action, and enable robust solutions.

ENGAGING SELF-RESPONSIBLE PEOPLE

The rules-based operating system is what most of us know well. For the past 100 years, industrial-style leaders have been trained to motivate and control people. Moreover, despite the wealth of research proving that there's no meaningful relationship between bonuses and performance, extensive extrinsic and monetary rewards continue to dominate people management. Stretched goals tied to incentives are the predominant means of change-based operating systems.

The fact is that rules-based systems achieve exactly what they're intended to: fulfilment of detailed objectives, and not one bit more. As management expert Peter Drucker once said: "Management by objectives works – if you know the objectives. Ninety percent of the time, you don't."

The engagement-based operating system demands personal mastery and meaning to engage people. We know from the philosophers of 17th-century European Humanism that self-responsible people are, by definition, motivated people. The engagement-based operating system is built on the assumption that people are fundamentally motivated and, as such, the management task is to help employees find that purpose. As we said earlier, this is called sense-making, not sense-giving.

High-performance sports professionals around the world know that engaged people need four things to perform at their peak:
1. They must be able to focus their attention on what matters most to them.
2. They need a high degree of awareness of what's most important.
3. They trust their own skills and their environment.
4. They require choice.

Choice is a prerequisite for self-responsible behaviours. If you cannot say no, then you have no choice and, therefore, cannot be self-responsible. Managers are well advised to give this careful thought.

As an example, a renowned leadership think tank I worked with decided to invest in 'people engagement' activities, as recommended by mainstream consultants. No doubt, their efforts resulted in a better place to work. But the company lost on speed, agility and robustness. Meetings, town halls, and more personal conversations augmented the sense of purpose, but what truly mattered to the organization was whether employees could fully apply their talent and focus on priorities to actually get things done.

Insights from diagnostic mentoring revealed the need to complement engagement activities with a toolbox for 21st-century working practices. Less than two months after these practices were put in place at the organization, creativity increased, collaboration became a natural way of working, and relevant knowledge was shared and accumulated.

Self-responsible action and a deep sense of purpose enable people to use their time most effectively. As a result, organizations that embrace this approach get things done faster, and still have things under control, despite a more dynamic environment.

MAKING DECISIONS
BASED ON
COLLECTIVE WISDOM

With rules-based operating systems, decisions are made through hierarchy. Delegated decisions always require the manager's signature, which means the boss always makes the decisions. We know that most leaders understand that this type of top-down control makes organizations slow, inflexible and fragile.

In change-based operations, it's always the leader who decides, assuming that they're the most qualified and most knowledgeable in the organization. As the academic and business management author Henry Mintzberg would put it, in these organizations, people are seen as removable human resources, costly human assets, and human capital. They aren't seen as human beings who add value to an organization.

By contrast, engagement-based operations favour debate, reasoning and committees. People are valued for what they add: knowledge and experience. It's just that filling calendars with endless meetings doesn't add to the agility of these companies.

Capabilities-based operations favour decision-making through collective wisdom. Decisions are delegated to the most knowledgeable and skilled person. Rapid feedback ensures that individuals and organizations learn quickly and continuously improve their decision-making and implementation of these decisions.

A high-tech utilities provider I work with successfully transformed from a CEO-driven, decision-making style to a collective approach. The challenges of the energy sector – with decreasing investment in traditional energy sources and more in riskier new sources – demands that companies continuously sense what is politically acceptable, judge what is possible, and decide what is doable. As such, energy companies require ongoing sensing and debate, without 'losing it' to analysis paralysis.

With the help of diagnostic mentoring, the CEO of this particular company was able to change his approach and began to mobilize knowledge and insights from his executive team. This quickly transformed his team into a body that used its collective wisdom and made the entire company more people-centric, without it getting locked into decisions without choices.

COORDINATING
SELF-ORGANIZED WORK

With rules-based operating systems, the coordination of work happens through detailed processes. Every time naturally connected parts fall apart, these companies install further operating procedures.

With the change-based operating system, managers initiate change projects to reconnect parts that have become disconnected through recently added structures and accountabilities. Workshops, meetings, alignment, and role clarifications are the means to coordinate work with the engagement-based operating system.

The capabilities-based operating system supports companies with decentralized businesses. Self-organized teamwork and ad-hoc project teams are favoured over strictly following plans and budgets.

Pharmaceutical firms I work with have long-established project teams that develop assets from research, development, distribution, marketing, and sales as parts of their business. Functions allocate knowledge and experience throughout the course of flexible and temporary projects. People mutually adjust in a self-organized and purpose-driven manner to release their productive energy. In this way, they help their organization remain flexibly grounded, with a stable backbone.

Self-organized work and mutual adjustment helps employees focus their attention on what matters most. A high degree of agility comes from the fact that shifting focus within a shared purpose makes organizations flexible.

THRIVING PERFORMANCE THROUGH BROAD PURPOSE

Rules-based operating systems apply rigorous individual management by objectives, with top-down goals and frequent performance appraisals. People in these modes spend a lot of time getting agreement on and conducting reviews of the performance objectives.

Change-based operations favour action orientation. In other words, valuable management time is dedicated to aligning value-adding projects and coordinating actions. These companies argue that implementation is what makes or breaks performance.

In engagement-based organizations, knowledge-driven employees follow their self-interest, making it difficult for management to get into balance with corporate intent.

People working in capabilities-based operating systems support teams with a shared mindset and clarity, based on broad direction, with a strong, shared purpose. Managers help them understand and use their energy to apply their full talent.

The public transportation company we recently worked with had transformed from a government agency to an independent entrepreneurial unit. One of the legacies it brought along was the rigid management-by-objectives system that dominated most management conversations. It was good practice to be very detailed and concrete when it came to target setting. A review of the organization's toolbox with the diagnostics revealed that rigorous and detailed routines made the entire company slow, inflexible, and fragile, like every other bureaucratic public administration.

By focusing people on 'serving their clients' – striving to offer the city's residents the world's best public transportation system – it unlocked the energy of its talent. This led to an entrepreneurially driven organization that was no longer weighed down by the negative effects of detailed targets.

Organizations with capabilities-based systems are able to release their productive energies through a broad sense of purpose, cooperation and high connectivity. These are the features of highly resilient businesses.

HYBRID OPERATING SYSTEMS

Throughout this book, I have argued for four dominant operating modes to establish a theory on operating systems. However, the diagnostic results of organizations reflect business reality. That reality hardly ever fits the pure theory. Hybrid modes are what we find in practice. The question is what this implies for operating systems.

Operating modes translate into operating systems through choices on the toolbox. The toolboxes for rules-based and capabilities-based differ widely. For example, leadership interaction with self-responsible people is supportive and encouraging. Alternatively, leadership interaction in the rules-based mode leverages hierarchy, with the purpose of checking on people. The capabilities-mode is all about helping people focus their attention, whereas control works on setting and controlling performance targets. The differences could not be greater. It is obvious that this requires resolve in order to not create tension or stress, and eventually leads to the use of an erroneous system or promote faulty leadership.

I have extensively documented faulty leadership, missing leadership – as well as out-of-control and erroneous systems – in *People-Centric Management*. These modes are not viable options. But they are not the same as dual operating systems. This leaves us with the question of merging operating systems or maintaining two (what we call dual operating systems). It's a big question indeed, as it arises from the discussion about exploitation and exploration business systems and their demands on management models and operating modes. The topic has received increasing attention in practice and in research. Following is my position on a diverse discourse.

Merging operating systems in a hybrid toolbox creates confusion. Target setting and focus of attention are opposites that don't align well. It takes sophisticated leadership and employees to do both. The experience is generally not very promising.

Selecting one operating system is a valuable option, and it must be the capabilities-based toolbox. Capabilities-based can also handle rules-based.

But rules-based cannot handle capabilities-based operations. Therefore, the capabilities-based toolbox is an honest choice. Experience shows that the capabilities-based toolbox renders superior results in the rules-based mode – beyond what the control can ever accomplish.

This leaves us with the last option: the dual operating system. That option is a deliberate choice to maintain both operating systems, acknowledging that some people operate in the rules-based mode and others in the capabilities-based mode. That is a condition for the dual mode. As such, there is a toolbox for leadership in the rules-based mode and one for the capabilities-based mode. This means that leaders need to be proficient at understanding and operating in both modes. It's obvious that collaboration, employee engagement, motivation, and control require more energy for leadership and work than normal. People need to function in an ambidextrous operating environment. Experience shows that this works, although it's not easy.

I have made the case for the rules/capabilities-based modes. The same principles hold for any other combination of modes. Readers may follow the same analytical logic via levers, and their implications on operating systems, to find out whether their combination is feasible. Our diagnostic tool offers utmost clarity on your current mode and the options to consider. The experience of diagnostic mentors is valuable, as they have insights through practice cases on the specific choice of options. That limits the risks considerably on a key concept of diagnostic mentoring – the thought that business models, management models, and operating systems need to match if peak performance is the goal.

Given the desirability of high efficiency and high innovation, hybrid contexts and dual operating modes, ambidextrous contexts are more common in business reality than we think. I need to add the following: in an ambidextrous, hybrid, dual mode, it is more important than in any other mode to sense early signs of dysfunction, erroneous systems, or faulty leadership. That's where diagnostic mentoring comes back into play, with its emphasis on raising awareness, acting on insights, and learning fast.

It's time now to select your dominant operating mode and system.

- Are you clear about your dominant operating system?

If your answer is no, what can you do?

- Discuss the options with your team.
- Talk to a diagnostic mentoring expert.

The following, Chapter 16, brings you to the right design of the toolbox.

SELECT YOUR OPERATING SYSTEM

Better Management requires a dedicated operating system. Rules-based, change-based, engagement-based, and capabilities-based are the generic options. Hybrid modes and dual operating systems balance exploitation and exploration.

KEY CHAPTER IDEAS

- Every organization has its own, distinctive operating system.
- Operating systems create a shared language and a shared way of managing people and organizations.
- Four generic operating systems cover different contexts and managerial responses.
- Every operating system comes with a distinct culture, leadership interventions, and managerial systems.
- Hybrid modes require combination of operating systems.

ACTION AGENDA

- Clarify your preferred operating system and features you would like to have in line with your operating mode and business model priorities.

FURTHER READING

Michel, L (2020). *People-Centric Management: How Managers Use Four Levers to Bring Out the Greatness of Others*. London: LID Publishing.

CHAPTER

16

DESIGN THE TOOLBOX

Every organization has its toolbox. It includes leadership and systems elements. Four generic toolboxes serve as the starting point for the design of your own, unique toolbox. The design follows people-centric and dynamic features that enable the fitting of your toolbox.

THE TOOLBOX

Every operating system includes a toolbox (Figure 35) with leadership intervention mechanisms and managerial systems. Leadership and systems are the two control mechanisms leaders have available to influence the performance, behaviours and actions of people. Managers either then directly interfere to alter performance or they use systems in place that indirectly govern the performance of people. Leadership involves different interaction mechanisms. Systems come as rules, routines, and tools.

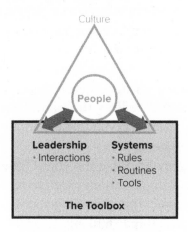

FIGURE 35: THE TOOLBOX

LEADERSHIP

Leadership is about interactions and includes sense-making, strategy conversions, performance conversations, contribution dialogue, and risk dialogue.

- **Sense-making**: Do leaders and employees have the ability to sense changes in internal and external environments and interpret their meaning?
- **Strategy**: Do leaders and employees have an understanding of why the organization has established strategic goals and are goals founded on lessons from the past?

- **Performance**: Do leaders and employees have a clear understanding of whether the organization is on track, what needs to be done to remain on track, and how to achieve superior performance?
- **Contribution**: Do leaders and employees have a clear understanding of what they can do to move the organization forward? As part of that, do leaders clearly understand their role?
- **Risk**: Do leaders and employees have a clear understanding of the potential risks and the ultimate level of risk the organization can tolerate?

RULES

Rules include the measurement system, strategic management, performance management, employee engagement, and governance.

The measurement system: How do we know? Measurement defines the model of how organizations think about performance. Dynamic measurement engages metrics beyond traditional financials, with a model that reflects the value creation of the entire business. Engage key people in your organization to define and apply your measurement system.

Strategic management: What direction? Strategic management refers to the approach organizations use to select their opportunities and challenges. Dynamic strategic management follows a model that enables delegated structured thinking. It establishes a shared language for how people think about their business and enables them to define and articulate strategy.

Performance management: What is our model? The main purpose of performance management is to implement the strategy. Self-organization demands a model that enables teams to manage their own performance. In a dynamic context, continuous planning and review based on relative goals beats traditional top-down budgeting.

The engagement system: How to get the mileage? Traditional engagement models focus on performance targets and incentive plans. Dynamic engagement systems are based on motivated people who want to deliver performance. Performance targets and rewards are applied at team or unit levels rather than given to individuals.

Governance: How to set the rules? In a dynamic environment, governance rules are defined as principles rather than strict operating procedures. This allows for entrepreneurial action rather than adherence to edicts. Social control replaces management action.

ROUTINES

Routines include the following: Information and feedback, strategy development, performance planning, and business reviews, objectives alignment, and risk management.

Information and feedback: How to create meaning? Information and feedback is the process by which people gain a deep understanding of what's going on. Access to relevant information and feedback, directed to where the work is being done, creates meaning.

Strategy development: How to create the strategy? Strategy development guides the thinking. Dynamic strategy development is about innovation and new opportunities. Make it a continuous process that engages key people, not simply the topic of a once-a-year offsite executive meeting. Rather than cascading strategy downward, enable delegated decision-making in teams, allowing them to create their strategies.

Performance planning and business reviews: How to implement? In a dynamic context, strategy (the thinking) and implementation (the doing) are not separated. They are one continuous process that links hierarchical levels and seamlessly coordinates with related departments. Dynamic planning and review are by no means out of control. On the contrary, they enable peer-control through rigorous business reviews.

Objectives alignment: How to coordinate? In a hierarchical setting with performance targets and incentives, the downward cascading of objectives takes up considerable management time. People-centric demands the alignment of goals among departments that need to work together. In that way, objectives become the means to coordinate and align with the firm's goals.

Risk management: How to avoid the undesired? Risk management is often seen as a once-a-year executive assessment of the company's overall risks. In a dynamic context, risks are assessed continuously. It's a learning process that attempts to see the invisible and raise awareness of the organization's boundaries.

TOOLS

Tools include performance indicators, strategy, performance plans and reports, vision, values, contribution and benefits, mission, risk, and structures.

Performance indicators: What metrics? Key performance indicators (KPIs) steer attention to what truly matters. Limiting performance indicators to seven, so people can easily memorize them, helps with selecting those metrics that must be kept in mind.

Strategy: What direction? In simplest terms, strategy defines the value that the business promises to its stakeholders – clients, employees, suppliers, the public, and shareholders. The brand of the business attaches specific values to its promises. This is why a dynamic strategy establishes a strong relationship with people and a shared intent to move in one direction.

Performance plans and reports: What goals and steps? Dynamic plans and reports focus on action, not on financial projections. Rather than detailed targets, relative goals and actions are documented and reviewed regularly, based on two-page documents.

Vision, values, contribution, and benefits: What expectations? Ambitions work like magnets: they create effortless pull. Vision and values are important sources of energy. They help people focus their attention on what truly matters: their contributions.

Mission, risks and structures: What rules? Dynamic boundaries frame what is inside and what is outside the confines of the business. They help people limit their activities to the set boundaries without limiting entrepreneurship.

FOUR GENERIC TOOLBOXES

Figure 36 illustrates four generic toolboxes: combination of interactions, rules, routines, and tools with their function to serve the specific context (traditional, dynamic) and the approach to management (traditional, people-centric).

These are the ten most important tools based on our research with 400 organizations and their preferences.

	Dynamic	
	Change Management action	**Capabilities** Learning, development, and cooperation
	1. **Performance plans and report** (Change) 2. **Strategy** (Emergence, volatility) 3. **Vision/Values/Contrib./Benefits** (Complexity, incentives) 4. **Performance planning and review** (Targets) 5. **Risk dialogue** (Delegation) 6. **Sense-making** (Engagement, command) 7. **Risk Management** (Coordination) 8. **Contribution dialogue** (Mobilization) 9. **Performance indicators** (Uncertainty) 10. **Performance management** (Rules, ambiguity)	1. **Vision/Values/Contrib./Benefits** (Engagement, self-responsibility) 2. **Risk dialogue** (Delegation, uncertainty) 3. **Sense-making** (Self-organization, complexity) 4. **Performance planning and review** (Attention, collaboration) 5. **Objectives alignment** (mobilizing) 6. **Mission, structure, risks** (Coordination, teamwork) 7. **Strategic management** (Capabilities) 8. **Measurement** (Ambiguity, options) 9. **Contribution dialogue** (Volatility) 10. **Performance conversation** (Emergence)
	Rules Hierarchy and power	**Engagement** Individual knowledge
	1. **Sense-making** (Power, uncertainty, influence) 2. **Performance Plans** (Volatility, incentives) 3. **Target setting** (Coordination, targets) 4. **Performance Indicators** (Direction, KPIs) 5. **Risk dialogue** (Engagement, command) 6. **Performance feedback** (Control) 7. **Measurement** (Ambiguity, BSC) 8. **Vision/Values/Contrib./Benefits** (Coordination) 9. **Performance management** (Change) 10. **Performance planning and review** (Budgeting, reducing complexity)	1. **Objectives alignment** (Complexity) 2. **Sense-making** (Engagement, purpose) 3. **Performance management** (Efficiency, volatility) 4. **Risk dialogue** (Uncertainty, power) 5. **Performance plans and reports** (Bureaucracy) 6. **Vision/Values/Contrib./Benefits** (Mobilizing, attention) 7. **Strategy conversation** (Capabilities) 8. **Mission, structure, risks** (Teamwork, coordination) 9. **Performance indicators** (Attention) 10. **Governance** (Standards, ambiguity)
	Stable	

Context

Traditional   **Management**   People-centric

FIGURE 36: FOUR GENERIC TOOLBOXES

THE RULES-BASED TOOLBOX

This toolbox has a clear focus on performance, measurement, and targets. Sense-making, the top priority, indicates the preference of direct leadership interventions to determine plans, set targets, and manage through performance indicators. The risk dialogue is used to control and reduce uncertainty with critical decisions. Budgeting, at large, dominates through performance planning and reviews. Overall, the toolbox cements bureaucracy base on hierarchy and power.

THE CHANGE-BASED TOOLBOX

Tools dominate in the change-based toolbox. Plans, strategy, vision, contributions, and incentives separate the thinking, done by leaders, from the doing, performed by employees. The risk dialogue and sense-making serve as the bridge between leaders and employees. The composition of the toolbox signs clear management action.

THE ENGAGEMENT-BASED TOOLBOX

Prima donnas are hard to manage. Objectives alignment is used to coordinate expert knowledge and, at the same time, sense-making and performance management ensure that 'race horses' are motivated to deliver value. Leaders use a mixture of dialogues and controls to manage individuals. Incentives are meant to ensure that the organization gets the best value for the talent.

THE CAPABILITIES-BASED TOOLBOX

Self-responsible people are driven by purpose. Vision, values, contributions, and benefits are offered to people to find purpose in what they do. A combination of risk dialogue, sense-making, and plans are in place to ensure coordination and alignment of self-organized groups. Principles for measurement and strategic management are in place to support decentralized teams. Overall, more leadership intervention is in place as compared to rigorous routines that fully support the idea of learning, development, and cooperation.

The four toolboxes offer guidance for the design of your individual toolbox. Based on a sample of 400 organization, these are the toolbox options that worked well. But by no means are they a prescription for your own toolbox. You need to design your own based on your needs and the principles we have set forth in *Better Management*.

PEOPLE-CENTRIC AND DYNAMIC FEATURES

Digitalization changes the nature of work. New external challenges and the distribution of knowledge require a different toolbox. Better Management comes with a toolbox that helps people to use their knowledge, skills, and resources and simultaneously helps them to deal with rising challenges. This toolbox features agile, people-centric, and dynamic capabilities.

Figure 37 bridges people, organization and context at work to show the challenges of the outer game that people and organizations accept. The bridge offers four principles that combine people-centric and dynamic capabilities. Better Management recognizes a toolbox that follows all four principles.

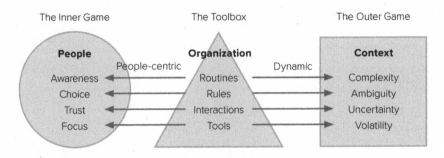

FIGURE 37: THE PEOPLE-ORGANIZATION-CONTEXT BRIDGE

There are four ways to bridge people, organization and context with a toolbox:

1. **To cope with growing complexity, routines need to create awareness more than control.** Complexity is like water, in that it cannot be compacted. Greater awareness is the only way to deal with increased complexity. Traditional ways to address complexity include decomposing it, setting goals, and delegating decision-making. Greater complexity is a frequent cause of bureaucratic routines and managerial processes

being ineffective. The fix is appropriate design that addresses the lack of rigour. Prevention is the design of routines that enable higher levels of awareness. The task is to decide on a learning policy with the appropriate balance between enabling learning and the need for control.

2. **In ambiguous environments, rules need to enable choice while they regulate the game.** When the future is unclear, choice in decision-making performs better than standard operating procedures. Greater ambiguity is a frequent cause of infected rules and the lack of discipline to follow them. Agility and speed in dealing with ambiguities requires a design for choice. Decide on your people policy and set your rules in a way that supports the right balance between self-determination and motivation by leaders.

3. **To cope with greater uncertainty, leadership needs to trust rather than command.** The only way to deal with uncertainties is to trust your own capabilities. With increasing uncertainty, it is important to define a leadership policy that balances responsibility and outside control. The fix for flawed leadership is an appropriate design of interactions for better relationships and collaboration. To prevent creeping uncertainty from hampering performance, interactions need a design with features to enable trust.

4. **To address changing dynamics, tools need to focus attention rather than aim.** When things change fast, people need something they can hold on to. Use tools that focus attention on what is important. With increasing volatility and changing market dynamics, it is important to get the control policy right, as a balance between enabling self-initiative and fostering goal-achievement. The fix for erroneous tools is their appropriate design for purpose and collaboration. Prevention is the use of tools that helps people focus their attention rather than just enabling control.

A toolbox that aligns with people's needs enables organizations to address a challenging environment. To close the dynamic gaps, organizations must equip their toolbox with people-centric features

– the features that enact the inner game. The management model and its levers offer the choice between traditional and people-centric principles. To enable people to address the challenges of the outer game, the toolbox requires dynamic features as a choice between stable and dynamic systems features.

To close the people-centric gaps of the current toolbox and enable dynamic features, the above four principles guide the design of all routines, rules, interactions and tools.

TOOLBOX
FITTING

Rules, routines, tools, and interactions equip the toolbox. The operating modes and the principles of the bridge between people, organization and context determine the purpose and features of the toolbox. Three action steps offer what I call 'toolbox fitting.' Four principles determine the choice of tools:

- The life cycle stage determines the choice of tools.
- Structure determines the choice of routines.
- Decentralization determines the choice of interactions.
- Type of organization determines the choice of rules.

The life cycle stage of an organization determines the choice of tools. In *Levers of Control* (1995), Harvard Business School Professor Robert Simons identified the evolution of management control systems over the life cycle of a firm. With this, and the Greiner (1997) life cycle model, Figure 38 suggests the following choices for an overlay of tools.

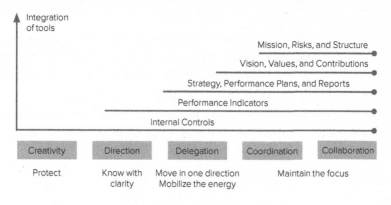

FIGURE 38: THE CHOICE OF TOOLS

Organizational structure determines the choice of routines. Organizations vary greatly in how they structure accountability for decisions and actions. The portfolio of managerial routines gets bigger as more routines are integrated to address the greater organizational complexity. Figure 39 lists the portfolio of routines for four different organizations.

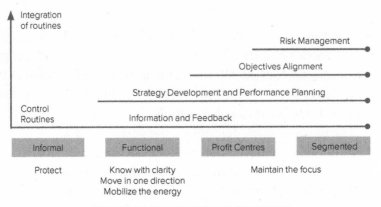

FIGURE 39: THE CHOICE OF ROUTINES

The degree of decentralization determines the choice of interactions. How organizations structure their decision-making varies from centralized to decentralized. In centralized organizations, decisions are made at the top. In decentralized organizations, decisions are made with employees at the client front.

With more knowledgeable employees at the client front, decision-making migrates to the periphery. Managers and employees need more time and energy to interact, share, align, and coordinate work. With this, the choice of interactions needs to take into account interdependencies and the distribution of knowledge. With increasing decentralization, the variety and integration of interaction mechanisms increases (Figure 40).

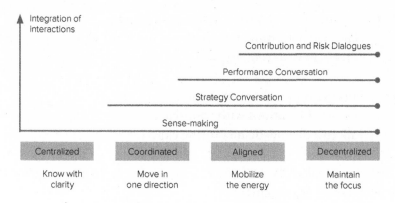

FIGURE 40: THE CHOICE OF INTERACTIONS

The unit of analysis determines the choice of rules. Not every organizational unit requires the same set of rules. The choice of rules varies from teams to departments, divisions, businesses, and conglomerates. Figure 41 shows the increasing integration of rules as units increase in size and complexity.

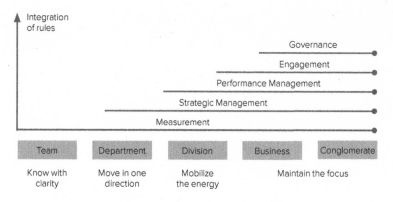

FIGURE 41: THE CHOICE OF RULES

With this, your next step is to design your toolbox.

- Have you determined the purpose, the features and the choice of tools in your toolbox?

If your answer is no, what can you do?

- Discuss the options with your team.
- Talk to a diagnostic mentoring expert.

The following, Part IV, introduces work *on* the system – it's how you develop Better Management.

DESIGN THE TOOLBOX

With clarity on the dominant operating system, it is time to design the toolbox. Better Management requires a toolbox that comes with people-centric and dynamic features. And it fits the demographics of the organization, life cycle stage, structure, degree of decentralization, and type of organization.

KEY CHAPTER IDEAS

- Rules, routines, tools and interactions compose a toolbox with 20 different elements.
- For each of the four operating systems, there is a generic toolbox.
- Every toolbox comes with people-centric and dynamic features.
- The choice of the toolbox fits the needs of the organization's life cycle stage, structure, degree of decentralization, and type.

ACTION AGENDA

- Clarify the features of your toolbox in line with your choice of operating system.

FURTHER READING

Michel, L (2021). *Diagnostic Mentoring: How to Transform the Way We Manage*. London: LID Publishing.

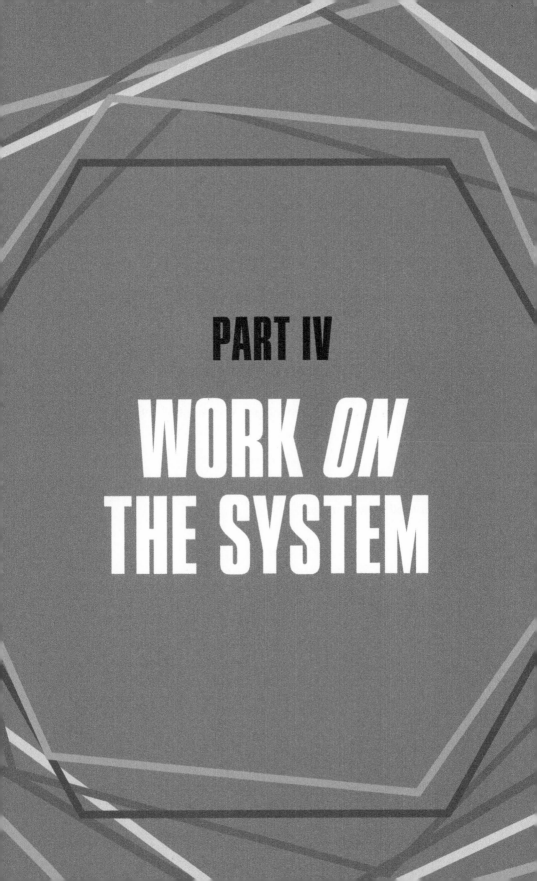

PART IV

WORK *ON* THE SYSTEM

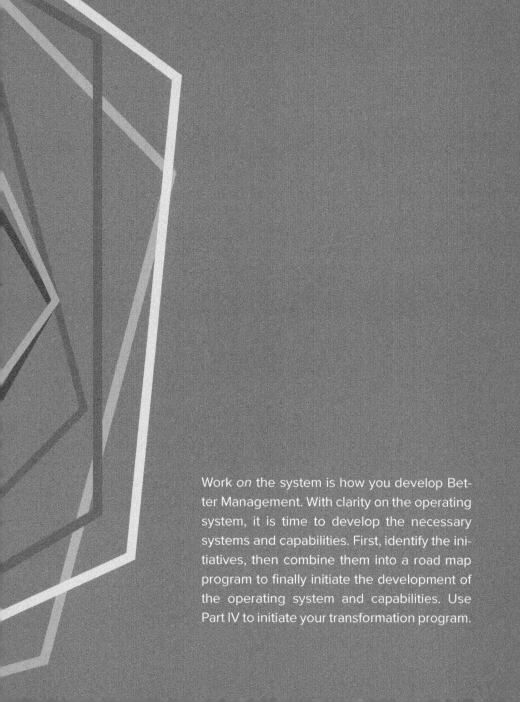

Work *on* the system is how you develop Better Management. With clarity on the operating system, it is time to develop the necessary systems and capabilities. First, identify the initiatives, then combine them into a road map program to finally initiate the development of the operating system and capabilities. Use Part IV to initiate your transformation program.

THE TIME IS NOW

When interference keeps the talent from performing, when a faulty operating mode gets leadership stuck, and when context changes, then it's time to work *on* the system of management. Most of the time, the shift to Better Management always happens while you work *in* the system. The risks of doing nothing are too big. The time to work *on* the system for Better Management is now.

THREE TRIGGERS

Three triggers initiate the transformation to Better Management. We often hear from executive teams that they "need to be more people-centric, agile, dynamic." Unless you've already made that decision, here are three triggers to help you get going. They ask for a change in the design of your operating system and management capabilities:

- **Interference and unused potential**: When your organization lacks performance.
- **Faulty operating mode**: When your leadership and systems are stuck in old modes.
- **Change in context**: When your business environment has changed.

INTERFERENCE AND UNUSED POTENTIAL

When interference and unused potential limit performance, it's time to consider an update of your operating system. You notice interference when your leadership requires lots of time to fix what should be normal. When fluctuation increases, it's time to look at unused potential.

Interference stems from erroneous systems, faulty leadership, or a virus-infected culture. All three require a fix. The fix may need a shift to people-centric – for example, tools in the toolbox that don't fit create undesired behaviours. Or self-responsibility and detailed performance targets don't fit. The results default to control, which limits motivation and engagement.

Unused potential is a major cost driver. It doesn't make sense to hire the best talent and then limit their engagement. Systems and leadership are a frequent cause of such inefficiencies. For example, control-oriented leadership may drive efficiency, but it limits creativity. As we noted earlier, when people take orders, they will follow those orders but do no more. As a result, organizations miss out on the creative potential and, eventually, the innovation capacity.

What do you fix first: leaders, culture, or systems? Imagine that you've decided to make the shift to people-centric, agile, and dynamic. Where do you start your intervention?

Culture? It is an outcome that requires interventions in leadership and systems. Over time, this will result in an effective culture.

Leadership? This is where most fixing starts. But why would you train leaders to come back in on Monday morning only to find themselves in the same mess?

Here is what works best: First, fix systems, and then train leaders to use them interactively. Over time, this will establish a strong shared culture. Remove systems interference before developing leaders.

In their *Harvard Business Review* article, "Why Leadership Training Fails – and What to Do About It," management consultants Michael Beer, Magnus Finnström, and Derek Schrader (2016) make the following point: "The problem was that even well-trained and motivated employees could not apply their new knowledge and skills when they returned to their units, which were entrenched in established ways of doing things. In short, the individuals had less power to change the system surrounding them than the system had to shape them."

Systems that define roles, routines, and rules have a strong impact on individuals' mindsets and behaviours. If the system does not change, it will set people up to fail.

FAULTY OPERATING MODE

When your business functions in the wrong operating mode, you can expect interference to take over and opportunities to be lost.

The degree of external challenges and the distribution of knowledge are the two triggers that determine the choice of your operating mode.

Rules-based and engagement-based modes work in a stable environment. A dynamic environment needs dynamic capabilities. And, knowledge-based management is rooted in the engagement-mode, with people-centric capabilities. Context and operations need to match.

CHANGE IN CONTEXT

When VUCA conditions change, it's time to adjust your operating mode.

For example, fixed performance targets and volatility don't go together. In a fast-changing context, annual goals prevent people from adapting to the change. Remember, targets are agreed upon, so they represent a contract between the employee and the organization. It's unfair to ask an employee to bend a contract and accept a disadvantage in order to follow the change. A system that works well in a stable environment may turn against employees and the organization when the context changes.

How do you know? Over the last 20 years, we've learned that it makes sense to diagnose your context and the operating system for viruses and unused potential. Such diagnosis offers a neutral outside perspective, with clarity on what requires change and how to initiate that development.

I also understand why it's hard to leave traditional approaches. Few leaders are willing to abandon their comfort zone for the chaos of uncharted territory. It's a risk. And the Dunning-Kruger Effect (Dunning, 2011) points to many leaders overestimating their own capabilities, and those of their organization, in making the shift. As a leader, self-confidence is essential; it is part of any leader's DNA. But overconfidence and being risk-averse are like boomerangs. Demotivation and the feeling that change is impossible spread like a virus in teams. That leader gets very lonely, giving rise to the conviction that it's the leader who has to do all the work. And so, there we are, stuck in a vicious cycle.

MAKE THE SHIFT

Diagnostic mentoring is work on the system, based on experiential learning and the inner-game technique. It applies the same principles as in working *in* the system: Better Management. Work *on* the system follows five activities (Figure 42): understand context, apply the inner-game technique, follow people-centric principles, design the toolbox, and make the shift to work *in* the system.

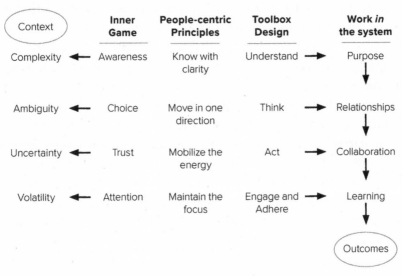

FIGURE 42: MAKE THE SHIFT

Every part requires your work on the system:

Understand context: With increasing VUCA challenges, agile, people-centric and dynamic capabilities help your organization quickly adapt to the new environment. They resolve the tensions between the challenges of the new context and the need for clarity, direction, energy, and focus. Chapters 1–5 are about raising awareness in your team that the context has changed, which launches the quest for Better Management.

Play the inner game: People are best equipped to resolve the tensions the new context poses. They apply four inner-game principles

– awareness, choice, trust, and attention – to address the challenges of the outer game. Chapters 6–11 outline your current choices base on the six principles of Better Management. Applying the inner game is a mindset question that has implications for the design of the operating system.

Design a dynamic toolbox: Following the principles of management design enables you to determine your operating system. Chapters 12–16 require you to make a decision on your toolbox with rules, routines, and tools that leaders in your organization can use at scale for Better Management. You will have to think about the right design of your operating system.

Work *in* the system: With the right design of your toolbox, your leaders can establish purpose as the source of motivation, connect people to nurture relationships, facilitate collaboration as a means to coordinate work, and expedite learning as the means to perform, innovate and grow.

Use diagnostic mentoring to get your team to design the dynamic toolbox that fits the people-centric approach and apply the principles to help you deal with a dynamic environment and deliver superior business outcomes.

With your personal shift to better management, you are ready to engage your team in the same way you've made your journey through experiential learning. Assume that your talents are motivated and want to learn to gain that experience fast. This learning involves an investment in the skills required to play the inner game, use resources the agile way and make better decisions. Architects, translators and doers will support you in the shift.

Experiential learning is the cycle that establishes leadership everywhere, develops agility, offers client focus, and drives performance. It applies the inner game (awareness, choice, trust, and focus) to build experience among your team. At the same time, it uses the inner game to lead the agile way. Understanding the principles of the inner game is easy. Applying them requires skill and dedication.

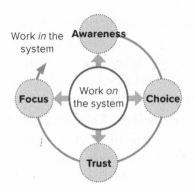

Work *in* the system

Awareness

Focus

Work *on* the system

Choice

Trust

FIGURE 43: WORK *ON* THE SYSTEM

Experiential learning (Figure 43) simultaneously involves work on the system and work in the system (see Chapter 1). Start in one place in your organization, and then expand the idea across all other units. Don't experiment – one does not experiment with people. Do it as a means to improve work, organization and management.

Better Management is the goal. Awareness initiates the learning, to get you started. People-centric is your choice of leadership style. It replaces traditional change, which never worked anyway. Trust your team to care about clients. Focus your attention for superior performance, innovation, and growth.

Experience is the opposite of education. It combines work on the system with work in the system. Don't try to educate your leaders through yet another executive development programme. Engage them in creating systems that support the transformation journey. To support your engagement, *Agile by Choice*, my previous book, offers 14 nudges to guide your team and wider organization to make the shift to Better Management.

THE RISKS OF
DOING NOTHING

Digitalization and the changing nature of work are the two trends that fundamentally challenge traditional management systems and organizational structures. Thy represent a silent revolution where the normal – what we have all learned – does not work anymore.

In the new, dynamic context:

- Managers can't tell people what to do.
- Control is exercised by letting go of control.
- Talent drives strategy.
- Implementation requires small teams and tasks.
- Complex systems must be scaled down.
- Companies make money by not focusing on money.

Current managerial operating systems and leaders, with 20th-century assumptions, are unsuited to handle these counterintuitive ideas. Digitalization and different work modes disrupt traditional operations. They're interferences. Businesses lose twofold as interferences reduce performance and unused knowledge limits potential.

When work systems change, management systems need to follow. Even in a traditional, stable environment, the risks associated with not doing anything are high. The clues come from five myths detailed in "Why Strategy Execution Unravels – and What to Do About It" (Sull, Homkes and Sull, 2015), an extensive study on implementation practices.

Myth 1: Implementation equals alignment. Managers use objectives, cascading objectives, measuring progress, and rewarding performance as their traditional ways to align with strategy. When asked how they would improve implementation, they generally said with more of the same tools, such as 'management by objectives' and 'balanced scorecards.' And most executives would argue that their organization is good at alignment. So why, then, are companies struggling with implementation?

When asked about commitments, 84% of managers say that they can rely on their bosses. But only 9% (Sull, Homkes and Sull, 2015) say they can rely on colleagues in other functions and units all the time. When managers cannot rely on colleagues in other parts of the organization, they duplicate efforts, let promises slip, delay deliverables, or pass up attractive opportunities – all dysfunctional, damaging behaviours.

However, even in companies with effective practices for cascading objectives throughout their hierarchies, the systems, and routines for horizontal coordination often lack teeth. Tools may be in place, but managers don't believe in them. Vertical dominates horizontal.

Myth 2: Implementation means sticking to the plan. For most managers, creating a strategy means establishing detailed plans that explain who should do what, by when and with what resources. Strategic planning and budgeting have long been the backbone of strategy implementation. Deviations from plans are seen as a lack of discipline that undermines implementation.

Unfortunately, fixed plans don't survive any dynamic reality. Managers need to adapt to the facts on the ground and overcome unexpected obstacles to capture valuable opportunities. Adjustments to reality require agility.

The lack of agility is a major obstacle to strategy implementation in most companies. A third of executives admit to difficulties in adapting to changing circumstances. But most organizations react so slowly that they miss opportunities. Just as managers want more structure and processes for coordination, they want more of the same to adapt to changing circumstances and flexibility in the allocation of resources.

Myth 3: Communication equals understanding. Many managers believe that relentless communication on strategy is important. Most would agree that they're clear about top priorities. But, when asked to name the top priorities, few can name just two. Not only are strategic objectives poorly understood, but they often seem unrelated to one another or disconnected from strategy. Fewer than a third of senior managers understand the connection between corporate priorities. Among supervisors and team leaders, that percentage is even lower.

The amount of communications is not the issue, as 90% of managers believe (Sull, Homkes and Sull, 2015) that top leaders communicate frequently. How can so much communication lead to such poor understanding? After all, the only thing that matters is what is being understood.

Myth 4: A performance culture drives implementation. When implementation fails, many managers point to a weak performance culture as the root cause. But implementation is rarely part of the official and explicit core values. However, it is an important part of the implicit culture when decisions need to be made on a day-to-day basis.

Past performance is the predominant factor when people decisions are made. But a culture that supports implementation must recognize other things as well, such as collaboration, agility, and teamwork.

The excessive emphasis on performance can hinder implementation in a subtle way. When making performance goals is most important, managers start gaming their performance commitments, and the result is mediocrity.

The most critical issue with many corporate cultures is that they reward performance more than coordination and collaboration. When asked about that, most managers would agree that sacrificing collaboration in favour of performance is acceptable.

Myth 5: Implementation should be driven from the top. A strong emphasis on top leaders negotiating performance objectives with their subordinates, and monitoring their progress, might work in the short term. It signals top-down implementation.

But most decisions in larger organizations are made at the client front, with leaders and employees who get the work done. Top-down management by objectives undermines what middle management and supervisors do in organizations. Delegated leadership shines.

Most middle managers live up the organization's values and goals most of the time. They do an especially good job reinforcing performance and holding teams accountable.

Many executives try to solve the problem of implementation – and with it, efficiency – by reducing complexity to one thing. They do a number of things: tighten the alignment up and down the hierarchy; stick to plans or ignore them; communicate frequently but with little understanding; focus on goal achievement; and look to the top when making decisions. This creates a culture full of viruses that interfere with implementation and performance rather than unlock the potential.

These myths are the hallmark of traditional management.

Leaders who manage with an operating system designed for analogue when digital takes over face daily interferences. This impacts employees, too, with mounting interferences and missing performance. When people with knowledge cannot engage and apply their talent, their talent is unused, and the business misses out on performance. With an interference-free operating system, people can put their talent to work. Knowledge is a capability that grows with its use. Engaging that knowledge must be in the interest of leaders, the business and all other stakeholders.

The risks of 'business as usual' are substantial and can include lack of performance, unengaged people, and missed opportunities. And this is regardless of whether businesses operate in a stable environment or a dynamic one. The solution is to have a managerial operating system without viruses, where people can unlock their talent to deliver sustainable performance – consistently, reliably, and robustly – with agile features.

Without management action, operating systems deteriorate over time (Figure 44). When the toolbox is outdated, then leaders first compensate the trend by increasing their direct influence. Work *out* of the system dominates, which in turn starts infecting the culture. Multiple individual toolboxes dominate and offer short cuts. The operating system further deteriorates. But there is a tipping point. When leaders are seen to compete with each other to get their work done first, then this directly leads to an infected culture. It is no more clear what rules, routines, tools, and interactions are within limits and what is out of the official boundaries. The spiral keeps turning negative.

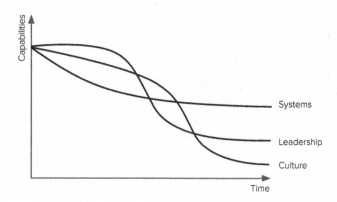

FIGURE 44: THE RISKS OF DOING NOTHING

The only management action is to invest in keeping the operating system current – in support of the people who need to get work done.

CAPABILITY MONITORING

Monitoring is the discipline to observe and alter capabilities. By observing (scanning) capabilities, potential faults and malfunctions can be spotted at an early stage. By becoming aware of critical signals, potential design requirements can be identified. With this, leaders can decide whether or not to address the issues. As such, monitoring initiates changes in capabilities.

Distance, new perspectives, critique, and multi-voice input are integral parts of the monitoring. Taking a step back, observing, and challenging the use of capabilities compensates for the risks of getting locked in. And so, organizations need to review their tools, routines, and behaviours in view of their specific context.

Monitoring is risk management. The use of managerial tools and processes is selective. For every context, leaders select the specific systems that support them in managing their organization in that specific context. When the context changes, the toolbox also needs to change. Diagnosing systems, leadership, and culture prevents organizations from misapplying tools, ignoring critical events, or being threatened by changes in their operating context.

Taking an arms-length stance, observation, and critique of design and capabilities helps compensate for risks, such as thoughtless reproduction of organizational designs and capabilities through path dependency, structural inertia, and lock-in. Early warning systems, including monitoring and reflection, can help reduce these risks. This first step, raising awareness, is such an early warning system.

People-centric principles, agile capabilities, and dynamic systems are not directly observable. They require indirect measurement. Monitoring as institutionalized, rules-based reflection is a nonroutine practice. If such monitoring is to succeed, it must be kept open; it must not become subject to closed-down routinization. Only then is it possible to detect extraordinary signals that call the validity of current design and capabilities into question.

Monitoring must include the internal and external environment. While internal factors can be identified, external factors are wide open and largely without boundaries. Crises are regularly preceded by weak signals. The interpretation of weak signals requires skills (Ansoff, 1980).

Design scanning and observation should follow systematic methods for generating, modifying, and improving capabilities. The monitoring routines themselves need to be updated repeatedly to prevent traps and path-effects. Professional agile insights diagnostics ensure effective monitoring, with continuous investments in the tool to prevent these traps.

It is important to encourage all units, subunits and individual members of an organization to actively participate in capability monitoring. Providing a supportive context and social climate is therefore a key task for effective monitoring. Leadership briefings establish the context and set the rules for a nonpolitical approach to design monitoring.

Capability monitoring is too costly to own and perform in-house for most organizations. Consequently, it makes sense to use an outside supplier with expertise, experience, and investment in professional diagnostics.

The time for Better Management is now. If not now, when then?

Now it's your turn to get started with your shift to Better Management.

* Are clear about the gaps and key issues to close the gaps with your operating system?

If your answer is no, what can you do?

* Revisit Chapters 6–11 to understand where you are and Chapter 15 to fix the basics.
* Consider diagnostic mentoring with capability monitoring as your approach.

The following, Chapter 18, helps you identify the initiatives.

THE TIME IS NOW

Work *on* the system alters the toolbox to adapt to the rising digitalization and the changing nature of work. When interference mounts, when the operating mode is ineffective, and when context changes, then it is time for an update of the toolbox.

KEY CHAPTER IDEAS

- Three triggers initiate a redesign of the toolbox.
- Successful managers first make their own shift to people-centric and agile.
- The risks of doing nothing is that your operating system deteriorates over time – unknowingly and unintentionally.

ACTION AGENDA

- Apply capability monitoring to scan your operating system in irregular intervals.
- Act on your insights and work on the operating system for Better Management.

FURTHER READING

Michel, L (2021). *Diagnostic Mentoring: How to Transform the Way We Manage*. London: LID Publishing.

CHAPTER
18

IDENTIFY THE INITIATIVES

The agile, people-centric, and dynamic capabilities shift is a transformation. Better Management is about scaling systems and individualizing leadership. To address higher challenges in the digital era, the operating system needs to handle a dynamic context and leadership needs to cater to every individual in the organization. In combination, that increases the agile capacity of the organization. To change from traditional to Better Management, disruption or evolution are the two choices. Your task is now to distil the initiatives with your team to enable that transformation.

IT'S A
TRANSFORMATION

Most diagnostic mentoring projects are a transformation. They alter the dominant paradigms in organizations. The shift from rules-based to capabilities-based is a paradigm shift to agile, people-centric, and dynamic capabilities (Figure 45). But there can be no shift without a stable platform to start from.

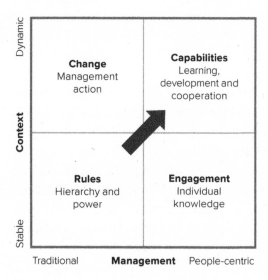

FIGURE 45: THE AGILE, PEOPLE-CENTRIC, AND DYNAMIC SHIFT

While control represents a stable platform with traditional managerial principles, enabling requires capabilities and tools with the ability to deal with a dynamic context. These new capabilities are in sharp contrast to traditional leadership and systems. It's a paradigm shift to a conscious new management mindset, set of skills, and toolbox.

A mindset shift usually means changing corporate culture. The new skills require leaders to learn new behaviours and decision-making styles. A new toolbox requires an operating system that helps leaders enable good work rather than control. Agile, people-centric, and dynamic are here to stay. It is the adaptive manifestation of management in a dynamic era. The people-centric shift requires a holistic transformation of capabilities and the toolbox, not just a quick fix on tools.

The shift to Better Management reconfigures resources that make a company different – those that are valuable, rare, and can't be substituted. In a dynamic environment, organizations need to constantly adapt their resource base. Agile capabilities offer the ability to select and use resources and competencies as processes that create, redefine, integrate, reconfigure, and renew capabilities to achieve new outcomes, such as greater agility in a fast-changing environment.

But Better Management is not limited to a dynamic environment. The paradigm shift is about better exploiting existing capabilities and the exploration of new capabilities. The shift balances stability with agility.

A stable platform with traditional principles in support of exploitation cannot simultaneously be agile and constantly change to enable exploration. A strong focus on stability reduces agile forces. Stabilizing and destabilizing require different processes; one process cannot perform both. Applying and selecting the right tools is about stabilizing. On the other hand, observation and reflection facilitate the learning for a dynamic context. They enable organizations to create a dynamic toolbox. In combination, stabilizing control and enabling require a design with agile capabilities.

As such, the shift not only develops and applies agile, people-centric, and dynamic tools, but it also deals with its inherent risks. It selects capabilities based on templates and patterns to solve the control problem, and it reduces the risks of dysfunctional viruses through early warning (self-reflection). With the agile, people-centric, and dynamic shift, capabilities emerge through learning as a routine that frequently deals with change of capabilities and innovation. Design requires selection of the right systems and a learning process for the development of these capabilities. It offers rules for change, learning mechanisms to accumulate experience, and ways to articulate and codify knowledge.

For managers, the challenge of the shift is to build the new capabilities and tools without losing control. A shift always requires a stable foundation, so making the shift successfully will require clarity on the starting point.

In a report titled "How to Create an Agile Organization," the global consulting powerhouse McKinsey (2017) argues that agile organizations excel at both stability and dynamism. Moreover, the report convincingly spotlights 18 dynamic practices that outperform stable practices in most aspects of strategy, process, structure, people, and technology. Traditional organizations can improve performance by applying agile capabilities.

With a successful shift to people-centric principles, agile capabilities and a dynamic operating system, the new mindsets, skills, and tools become an advantage. Such agile capabilities and dynamic systems are unique, and therefore difficult to copy. They are the foundations for a sustainable competitive advantage.

More than not, the shift is a transformation.

SCALING AND INDIVIDUALIZING

Scaling and individualizing the operating system prepares management for hybrid modes, with dual enabling dynamic features, while offering stability and efficiency. Agile, people-centric, and dynamic features combine scaling and individualizing.

In the previous section, on the quest for a new paradigm, we distinguished between a stable platform and a dynamic one. A hybrid context exists when organizations experience a stable and a dynamic context or operate with parts that are stable and dynamic. A hybrid context also exists when events or parts of the organization require control and others demand agile responses at the same time. Managers have a choice. They can operate in two different modes with two operating systems, or they can operate in a dual mode, with a dual operating system that can handle both. Scaling and individualizing offer a solution for dual operating systems. It also helps to have the choice of maintaining two separate operating systems and the capabilities necessary to switch between the two.

Systems offer the rules, routines and tools that help us operate in our specific context. Leadership interaction is how we use systems to support individuals, teams, and networks in applying their knowledge and getting work done.

Scaling adds dynamic features to efficiency, where people need to deal with increasing VUCA conditions. Talented people are all different. They come with different ambitions, talents, and skills.

Individualizing leadership adds people-centric to efficiency in ways that help every individual unlock their talent and contribute to create value.

Figure 46 frames scaling as a vertical intervention that requires dual systems and individualizing as a horizontal intervention in how we use dual systems in support of leadership.

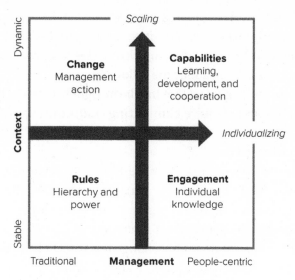

FIGURE 46: SCALING AND INDIVIDUALIZING

SCALING SYSTEMS

The challenge for organizations that operate in a hybrid mode is to scale management with an operating system that spans the entire organization. Hybrid modes demand the dual systems' features of traditional, people-centric, or dynamic. People-centric and agile can also do traditional.

Rules and Change-based: If you are an organization with a stable platform, but need to speed up change to reduce costs, drive immediate profitability, and strengthen competitive advantage, you need to mobilize resources and facilitate self-organization by showing trust in their implementation. That helps create a work environment that supports collaboration.

Engagement and Capabilities-based: If you're an entrepreneurial organization with highly engaged people but need to respond to rapid changes in the environment, be people-centric, and capture new technology-related opportunities, you need to delegate power to teams, tap into networks by providing direction, and facilitate everyone moving in one direction. That provides for a work environment that nurtures new relationships.

Stanford University management science expert Robert I Sutton articulated this in a *Harvard Business Review* article, "Eight Essentials for Scaling Up Without Screwing Up" (2014). He asserted that scaling management is all about the following:

- Spreading a mindset that instils the right beliefs and behaviours.
- Scaling may require eliminating traditions, strategies, practices, and roles that were once helpful but have outlived their usefulness.
- You have two choices: make people believers, and then let them freely localize the rituals, or legislate the behaviour you've identified as being best and assume that people will become believers and act that way.
- Rational arguments for change are insufficient; use positive emotions to channel energy and passion.
- Exposing people to leadership rhetoric is not enough; you should build or find excellence and use it to guide and inspire more excellence.
- Cut cognitive overload but embrace necessary organizational complexity.
- Build organizations where people come to feel, "I own the place, and the place owns me."
- Bad is stronger than good; clear away the things that stand in the way of excellence.

INDIVIDUALIZING LEADERSHIP

People who operate in a hybrid mode have a greater need for individual leadership. This is leadership that supports and interacts with learning, while at the same time offering clarity and the means to focus attention.

This can be achieved through:

- **Offering meaningful work**: Individualizing leaders focus on the why when they discuss work, goals, and projects. The idea is that employees come up with their own solutions to problems they're asked to solve.
- **Delegation and feedback**: Individualizing leaders have trust in people and teams, create an environment with degrees of

freedom along with a sense of safety, and offer feedback and support at eye level.

- **Learning in networks**. Individualizing leaders favour networks over hierarchies, and they enable learning in peer-to-peer contexts.
- **Balancing dual operating systems**. Individualizing leaders operate in ambidextrous ways that stretch between traditional and agile. They adjust their leadership style to what people and the context require, without losing consistency.
- **Leading virtually and enabling diversity**. Individualizing leaders interact face-to-face and digitally. They enable diversity by supporting heterogeneous teams.

In short, we're talking about individuals who search for purpose, connect and build relationships, naturally collaborate, and focus attention to learn. But learning is a shared responsibility between individuals and the organization, represented by its leaders. To individualize leadership, we need a dual operating system that combines traditional and agile interactions.

Rules and engagement-based: If you're a successful, well-positioned organization, but want to benefit from digitalization and tap into the knowledge of people, you need empowered employees who thrive on self-responsibility through information that raises awareness. They know with clarity, and that makes for a work environment where people find purpose.

Change and capabilities-based: If you're a flexible organization that's always reacting to changes in the environment, but you want to speed up learning, proactively capture opportunities, and align dispersed teams, you need to align the means and provide broad direction. This can be achieved through focus of attention, beliefs, and boundaries, allowing people to maintain focus. That makes for a work environment where they can learn.

Individualizing and scaling require ambidextrous capabilities from employees, leaders, and the operating system. Stress, conflicts, and role ambiguity limit the individual ability for ambidexterity. Diversity in leadership teams is a key factor in following an ambidextrous strategy. Leaders with a diverse background and teams with different experiences are more likely to explore new directions and capabilities while maintaining current operations. However, integrating individualizing and scaling functions in one responsibility tends not to work and, in fact, reduces overall ambidexterity. What works is individualizing leadership, and top management ensuring that managerial systems are designed to scale.

People-centric demands interactions with individuals. Interactions are an effective means of control. People-centric interactions are individual and specific to every person. The shift to people-centric demands that leaders be out at the client front, interact with stakeholders and 'interfere' as the means to exercise control. As interactions become more intense and take up a large part of senior executives' time, it makes sense to delegate (by a CEO) some of the organizing and planning work to a chief of staff, an assistant (by senior leaders) or junior managers (by other leaders). They can give you time to be with your people at the client front. Chiefs of staff can triage data and feed to leaders what they need in order to lead.

Scaling and individualizing are two complementary features of a dual operating system for organizations wanting to make the shift, operate in a hybrid mode and enable people-centric management. Scaling addresses the systems to operate in a dynamic environment, and individualizing updates leadership in the context of distributed knowledge. Intervention in any operating system is a transformation, as it alters the behaviours, decisions, and actions of people in organizations.

TWO INTERVENTION PATHS

So far, we have explored scaling and individualizing as concurrent interventions to make the shift to agile, people-centric and dynamic. However, there are two alternative paths that set different priorities for the intervention: disruption or evolution.

Figure 47 outlines both intervention paths. Disruption as an intervention first alters systems to scale agility, and then develops leadership to individualize people-centric management. Conversely, evolution first trains leaders on Better Management, and then scales Better Management throughout their organizations.

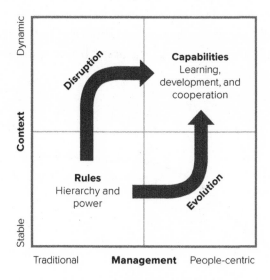

FIGURE 47: TWO INTERVENTION PATHS

It's a choice with different assumptions. Disruptions assume that behaviours change through altering the rules, routines, and tools for people to get work done. And they assume that once these systems are designed to address a dynamic environment, it's time to train leaders on the use of systems to enable Better Management.

On the contrary, evolution assumes that leaders with the right attitude and mindset can engage in Better Management and then change systems for a dynamic context.

Philosopher and organizational behaviour author Charles Handy, in his seminal book *The Second Curve*, introduced an S-shaped curve as a means to project the future. The S-shape indicates an initial period of investment, when input exceeds the output. As you begin to show results and progress is made, the line moves up. But there is inevitably a time when the curve peaks and begins its descent. The good news is that there's always a second curve. Disruptive innovations (Christensen, 2015) create that second curve.

Traditional management (Figure 48) evolved along the first curve over the past 100 years. It was a success story during a period of relative stability. People-centric management is the second curve – one that disrupts the traditional and will continue to evolve. When speed is important, but systems and processes slow you down, you know that disruption has arrived. Management, organization, and leadership are at an inflection point between traditional and Better Management.

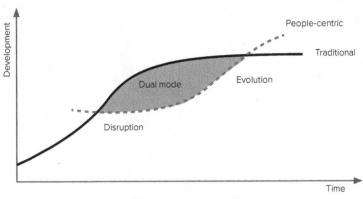

FIGURE 48: DISRUPTION AND EVOLUTION

Dynamic disrupts traditional management, but traditional will continue for a while. In fact, efficiency and reliability attributes will be needed more than ever to delight customers. Neither will go away altogether. The transformation means that both traditional and dynamic will coexist and perform as intended: traditional for exploitation and dynamic (agile) for exploration. This coexistence will require the hybrid mode of operations with a dual operating system.

Over time, evolution replaces disruption. The transformation mode shift will take you from adopting the operating system to training leaders and employees how to be effective in the agile mode. Training and education will do the job. But Harvard Business School's Amy Edmondson (2018) suggests that organizations need 'fertile soil' in place before 'seeds' of training interventions can grow. And, she notes, people need a sense of 'psychological safety' at work for transformations to succeed.

Can you first evolve and then disrupt? While companies spend billions annually on training and education (Beer, Finnström, and Schrader, 2016), the evidence of success is slim. Why do they continue what clearly doesn't work?

First, organizations are viewed as aggregations of individuals. By that logic, people must be selected and trained on the right skills, knowledge, and attitudes. The expectation is that this then translates into changed organizational capabilities. But organizations and systems consist of interconnected subsystems and processes that drive behaviour and performance. If systems don't change, they won't support individual behaviour change. Second, it's hard to confront senior executives with the uncomfortable truth that failure to change or implement isn't rooted in individuals' deficiencies, but in the policies and practices created by top management.

INITIATIVES

The six principles of Better Management (Chapters 6–11) offered the opportunity for you to evaluate your operating systems with competitive advantage as the benchmark in mind. This provided you with the gaps of your current operating system. Chapters 14–16 offered the key issues for the proper design of the operating system that now require your attention.

Initiatives are bundles of activities that translate key issues into initiatives that, in return, help you address the gaps. More than not, these key issues require a transformation that involves scaling systems and individualizing leadership.

From our experience we have learned that successful transformations come with five to seven initiatives.

What are my initiatives? Here are the questions to ask:

People: What initiatives unlock the potential for higher performance?

Organization: What initiatives remove the barriers to innovation?

Work: What initiatives leverage resources for superior growth?

Operations: What initiatives expand the potential to cope with a dynamic environment?

Management: What initiatives develop Better Management with the ability to capture higher challenges?

Now it's your turn to answer these questions with your team.

- Do you have a list of initiatives to initiate your transformation?

If your answer is no, what can you do?

- Continue to develop five to seven initiatives with your team.
- Consider diagnostic mentoring as your approach.

The following, Chapter 19, helps you determine the road map plan.

IDENTIFY THE INITIATIVES

The shift to Better Management is a transformation. The new operating system needs to support a dynamic context and distributed knowledge. The transformation may follow disruption or evolution. Initiatives articulate five to seven themes that facilitate the transformation.

KEY CHAPTER IDEAS

- Changes in the operating system that alter the behaviours, decisions and actions of people are a transformation.
- Scaling transforms the operating system to become dynamic.
- Individualizing transforms the operating system for people-centricity.
- There is choice for the transformation: disruption or evolution.
- Initiatives bundle the activities for the transformation.

ACTION AGENDA

- Apply diagnostic mentoring with your team to translate gaps and key issues into initiatives.

FURTHER READING

Michel, L (2021). *Diagnostic Mentoring: How to Transform the Way We Manage*. London: LID Publishing.

CHAPTER

19

DETERMINE THE ROAD MAP

The development of Better Management follows an individual development plan. Every organization is unique — so is every road map. The task is to create the program with your team based the assumption of knowledge work.

DISTRIBUTE DECISION-MAKING

While you determine the road map to Better Management, be reminded of the following: 'Knowledge work' means that people – not just leaders – have the full ability to act and make decisions. Distributed decision-making requires a people-centric operating environment in which people can apply their full potential. This is in sharp contrast to the traditional principles of the 'controlling mode', where interference prevents people from using their knowledge and experience to seize opportunities. In the enabling operating mode, the thinking and doing are united.

Knowledge work is made up of five control elements:

- **Understand**: Information and immediate feedback raise awareness of what is important. This helps people understand what matters and focuses attention. Superior understanding requires that sensors are not on mute and amplifiers work properly.
- **Think**: Knowledge workers have a set of mental maps that help them make sense of situations and make decisions. The benefits for an organization come not only from individual thinking but also from collective thinking. The thinking requires an opportunity to create meaning and asks for a deliberate choice to move in one direction.
- **Act**: This involves translating ideas into action. The task is to mobilize resources to get things done. People put their energy into things that they care about. And energy requires action to be meaningful. Contribution requires the opportunity to apply knowledge, and to support and balance freedom and constraints. Superior contributions build on trust of people and in people.
- **Engage**: Attention is a limited resource; energy is required to maintain it at a high level. Attention must be focused to prevent distraction from competing demands. The energy flows to where there is attention. A high level of engagement requires beliefs, motives, and purpose.

- **Adhere**: Energy adds pull and a positive tension to the boundaries of an organization. It helps traverse the stretch between safely staying within the boundaries and searching for opportunities outside the boundaries. This tension requires a balance between efficiency and entrepreneurship. A high level of adherence maintains a good balance.

Figure 49 contrasts traditional and better approaches to knowledge work according to these five elements.

	Understand	Think	Act	Engage	Adhere
In a people-centric context ...	Use information to get work done	Make decisions	Are motivated by a sense of purpose	Have clear priorities	Are empowered and clear about norms
People use their potential	Unlimited information	Unlimited opportunities; encouraged to take risks	Increased pressures	Limited attention; limited resources	Growing temptations for outside the boundaries
In a traditional context ...	Information is limited to the top	Leaders make decisions	Leaders motivate for performance	Employees execute ...	... and control what gets done
People are bound by limitations	Lack of information	Lack of opportunities; fear of risk	Lack of purpose	Conflicting goals; lack of resources	Lack of boundaries

FIGURE 49: KNOWLEDGE WORK

Better Management assumes a mindset where people want to contribute, develop, and work in a goal-oriented way. This is in sharp contrast to traditional assumptions where people are motivated, controlled, and trained. Figure 50 illustrates the differences for employees and leaders.

Better assumptions	Traditional assumptions
Knowledge employees ...	*As compared to ...*
Want to contribute	Don't do anything on their own
Want to do things right	Need to be developed
Want to achieve	Need to be directed
Want to be creative and develop	Do what they are told
People-centric managers ...	*As compared to ...*
Ask questions and focus	Motivate and decide; tell people what to do
Shape the environment	Judge and review
Support creativity	Sit at the top; provide instructions
Establish relationships	Are responsible; have the power to change and set the rules

FIGURE 50: THE ASSUMPTIONS

In a people-centric and dynamic context, managers have a new role: to create an environment where people can unlock their full talent.

FOUR SHIFTS

The road map to Better Management has four parts: the shift to purpose, relationship, collaboration, and learning (Figure 51). Each part requires the development of a distinct operating environment with a distinct culture, distinct leadership, distinct system – all based on agile, people-centric, and dynamic principles.

FIGURE 51: FOUR SHFTS

The purpose shift: The goal of the organization shifts from making money to delighting the customer. The role of the manager now is to help people find purpose, rather than telling them what to do.

The relationship shift: The relationship of individuals to their direct manager shifts to teams with delegated responsibility. And, with that pivot, the role of the manager is to offer direction and enable a supportive work environment, not to check on people's work.

The collaboration shift: Instead of work being coordinated by bureaucracy with rules, plans, and reports, it's coordinated through self-organization and agile approaches.

The learning shift: Rather than preoccupation with goals, efficiency, and predictability, now transparency, learning, sharing, and continuous improvement help teams maintain their focus.

THE PURPOSE SHIFT

The first shift is the story of people who know with clarity and find purpose. It's the shift from command to self-responsibility, with the goal of delighting the customer.

Command assumes that people need guidance to get things done. That guidance may range from detailed orders and control of actions to gentle observation. But both remain part of the traditional control mindset. It comes with traditional 'plan, do, check, and act' management skills that are guided by extensive performance measurement and information tools.

By contrast, self-responsibility builds on motivation. By definition, self-responsible people are motivated by the ability to say no to things. They're driven by purpose that guides their engagement. By agreeing to get things done by their own will, they'll apply their creativity and knowledge to better deal with greater complexity.

The first shift (Figure 52) enables people to find purpose. It requires a different mindset – a new set of skills and enabling tools that build on distributed knowledge for a dynamic era.

Management	From Traditional	To Better
Principle	Command	Self-responsibility
Culture	Hierarchy	Shared understanding, awareness
Leadership: sense-making	Control	Interactive sense-making for feedback and clarity
Rule: measurement	Budget review	Self-control
Routine: information and feedback	Restricted, limited to the top	Accessibility and transparency
Tool: performance indicators	Many detailed metrics	Few relevant outcome metrics

FIGURE 52: PURPOSE – FOR A DEEP UNDERSTANDING

The mind shift to self-responsibility: Self-responsibility is the prerequisite for motivation. It requires that leaders let go of traditional control modes. In a context where knowledge is widely distributed, agile assumes that people want to contribute and perform.

The shift to skills for feedback and sense-making: Motivated people demand purpose. They need feedback with information that helps them make sense. Agile demands active sense-making.

The shift of tools that deepen the understanding: Agile works with a toolbox that raises awareness of what matters most and creates a shared understanding.

Better Management builds on a strong, stable foundation. And then, a successful shift to self-responsibility always builds on solid capabilities that enable people to know with clarity. The stability comes from skills and tools to assess market moves and performance indicators that offer reliable feedback. Without high quality diagnostic information, it's a risky shift and agility remains fragile.

THE RELATIONSHIP SHIFT

The second shift is for people to move in one direction and build relationships to enhance knowledge. It's a shift from power to delegated responsibility in teams.

Power originates from a mindset with an industrial background of low-skilled work, where people need to be told what to do. It implies hierarchy and concentrated knowledge at the top. Relationships are formed through pre-set structures and formal authority. Power is exercised in many shades of grey, and it's important to note that power and authority are neither bad nor good. There are times when power and authority are the only way to get things done fast.

Delegation assumes that knowledge is widely distributed and those who assume responsibility know what they are doing. Choice is left to those who assume delegated responsibility. The challenge comes from the need to move in one direction. Alignment with strategy must come from intense conversations and sharing, which establish productive relationships.

The relationship shift (Figure 53) enables people to build relationships. It requires a new set of conversation and interaction skills that help transcend the shared intent throughout the organization.

Management	From Traditional	To Better
Principle	Power	Decentralization, delegation, teams
Culture	Personal agenda	Shared intent, choice
Leadership: strategy conversation	Top-down messaging	Interactive, encouragement to take risks
Rule: strategic management	Analysis	Modelling, testing
Routine: strategy development	Competitive advantage	Search for opportunities
Tool: strategy	A three- to five-year plan	Thinking, value proposition

FIGURE 53: RELATIONSHIP – TO ENABLE THE THINKING

The mind shift to delegation: Relationships at eye level work with distributed power, where people are accountable for their actions. Agile capabilities ensure that people move in one direction. As such, delegation offers a new and superior kind of control.

The shift to skills for strategy conversations: Delegation requires connectivity, sharing, and interaction. Agile capabilities, with conversations about strategy, enhance the employer brand and eventually employee loyalty.

The shift to tools that support the thinking: While traditional strategy tools focus on analysis, agile tools support delegated thinking throughout the organization. They offer choice and simultaneously enhance the bonding through a shared intent.

The shift from power to delegation does not mean that leaders lose control. Power is the stable platform from which the shift to delegation can be successfully made. Delegation demands interaction between leaders and employees on strategy and the way to get there.

THE COLLABORATION SHIFT

The third shift is of people who mobilize energy and collaborate across organizational boundaries. It's a shift from bureaucracy to coordination and collaboration in self-organized teams.

Bureaucracy builds on efficiency with leaders, rules, and routines to coordinate work. It works well with repetitive tasks that remain the same and where little collaboration is required. But we've also learned that trust is the fastest management concept around. Bureaucracy assumes a competitive environment where mistrust prevails. This is why there are alternatives to traditional bureaucracy.

Self-organization builds on natural trust and assumes that people at the client front are better equipped to coordinate where the work is being done. However, self-organization does not just happen. It requires energy from the outside in the form of leadership. But that leadership differs from traditional control. It comes with tools that enable teams to properly function in an uncertain environment.

The collaboration shift (Figure 54) enables people to collaborate with a new set of skills and tools that creates trust and a shared agenda throughout the organization.

Management	From Traditional	To Better
Principle	Bureaucracy	Self-organization
Culture	Plan-fulfilment, goal achievement	Resource flexibility, trust, shared agenda, value creation
Leadership: performance conversation	Planning	Interactive and dynamic coordination
Rule: performance management	Budgeting and resource allocation	Planning as continuous and engaging process
Routine: performance planning	Annual top-down budgeting	Just-in-time resource availability, rigorous (peer) business reviews
Tool: performance plans and reports	Fixed budgets, often linked to incentives	Relative goals

FIGURE 54: COLLABORATION – TO FOCUS ON DELIVERY

The mind shift to self-organization: It's a shift from fixed bureaucratic procedures to flexibility with resource allocation. Better Business capabilities ensure that resources are available on demand.

The shift to skills for performance conversations: Interactions across organizational boundaries enhance collaboration. People-centric, peer-review-based conversations focus on value creation rather than goal achievement.

The shift to tools that focus on delivery: Traditional management-by-objectives systems are replaced by business plans and reviews owned by self-organized teams. Planning and reviews facilitate collaboration with a shared agenda, based on trust, and replace top-down bureaucracy.

The shift from bureaucracy to self-organization enables collaboration throughout the organization. Bureaucracy adds the stable platform with rigorous routines, while self-organizations provide the flexibility of combining resources. A successful shift builds on a stable platform.

LEARNING SHIFT

The fourth shift is the story of people who maintain the focus and learn. It's the shift from preoccupation with narrow targets to enabling teams to maintain their focus through learning, sharing, and continuously improving.

Narrow targets limit the scope of action beyond team assignments or job descriptions. They're time-limited goals, set by managers to drive performance. Goal setting may range from fixed targets set by leaders to a contract that's agreed upon with employees. Yet, it remains a tool that cannot cope with higher volatility. The negative effects of gaming the target-setting process are widely discussed in the professional literature.

Attention with broad direction, by contrast, offers space and enables people to focus on things that matter most to their clients. Focus of attention, at the same time, is a tool that helps people learn and improve upon what they're doing.

The learning shift (Figure 55) enables people to focus attention and learn. It requires a different mindset, with new tools that work well in a volatile environment where knowledge dominates.

Management	From Traditional	To Better
Principle	Narrow targets	Broad direction
Culture	Risk prevention	Shared beliefs and norms, accumulating knowledge
Leadership: contribution and risk dialogues	Control	Interactive interventions, performance, learning and joy, entrepreneurial decisions
Rule: engagement and governance	Performance targets, rules, and incentives	Shared value, social control, entrepreneurship
Routine: objectives alignment, risk management	Incentive plans	Trust in teams and self-control
Tools: vision, values, contributions, mission, risks, structures	Narrow objectives with wordy directives	Focus of attention, base accountability on holistic factors and broad direction

FIGURE 55: LEARNING – TO FRAME ENGAGEMENT AND ADHERENCE

The mind shift to focus of attention: The primacy goes to seeing the whole rather than digging into all the detail. This is a shift away from goal setting with detailed, fixed targets; it's aimed at enabling people to focus attention within the frame of a broad direction.

The shift of skills to contribution and risk dialogues: These conversations zero in on how to maintain the focus rather than how to aim at goals. Focus directly impacts performance, whereas goals are an intellectual construct with no direct relationship to action.

The shift of tools to engage and adhere: Focus of attention enables learning. Agile tools establish the boundaries of the playing field, with beliefs and norms that frame entrepreneurial behaviours and actions. Broad direction and beliefs stretch the boundaries, whereas norms ensure that no one steps over the boundaries.

The learning shift changes leadership from applying detailed targets to communicating broad direction in support of entrepreneurial behaviours and actions. It assumes, however, that leaders have given some thought to the direction. A successful shift to people-centric builds on the stable platform that helps people maintain their focus and continuously learn.

THE ROAD MAP

The four shifts illustrate generic initiatives to Better Management. The road map combines initiatives into a comprehensive development programme that follows one of the paths.

The road map may include managerial interventions such as coaching, training, development, design, projects, workshops, experiments, events, and more. There is no limit, but it's an art to combine initiatives into a comprehensive programme that works. That's where experience is needed.

What is your road map programme? Here are the questions to ask:

People: What is our programme to leverage the potential, skills, knowledge, and resources of your people?

Organization: What is our programme to reinforce organizational competencies.

Work: What is our programme to alter the resources in support of the desired operating mode?

Operations: What is our programme to replace ongoing change with dynamic capabilities?

Management: What is our programme that turns Better Management into a competitive advantage?

Now it's your turn to answer these questions with your team.
- Do you have a plan to develop the systems and capabilities for better management?

If your answer is no, what can you do?
- Keep working to translate initiatives into a programme with your team.
- Consider diagnostic mentoring as your approach.

The following, Chapter 20, initiates the implementation of the road map with the development of the capabilities.

DETERMINE THE ROAD MAP

The road map is the plan to develop the capabilities and systems for Better Management. It translates initiatives into a program. Four generic shifts help you think through what your plan needs to look like. But be reminded of the essence of knowledge work.

KEY CHAPTER IDEAS

- The road map determines the program for the development of Better Management.
- Knowledge work is the foundation for Better Management.
- Four shifts outline what is needed to get to Better Management.

ACTION AGENDA

- Work with your team to translate initiatives into a development road map.

FURTHER READING

Michel, L (2021). *Diagnostic Mentoring: How to Transform the Way We Manage*. London: LID Publishing.

CHAPTER

20

INITIATE THE DEVELOPMENT

With the road map plan, it is time to initiate the development of agile, people-centric, and dynamic capabilities for Better Management. This chapter offers the learning opportunities to initiate the development.

THE DEVELOPMENT PROGRAM

The development program adds ideas and guidance to the road map programme. Agile, people-centric, and dynamic capabilities require different interventions. Figure 56 summarizes capabilities, development interventions, resources, and interventions. My previous books and other resources support the development in various ways.

Executive development engages managers in the inner game techniques for individual agility. Organizational development is the approach to develop agile at scale in organizations. People-centric management requires management development. Through systems development, managers design their toolbox. Leadership development then trains leaders in the use of systems.

Be aware, an estimated $60–$100 billion is spent worldwide on leadership development (Glaveski, 2019). The result of this investment is questionable: Managers feel dissatisfied with the development, it does not help to develop the skills for mastery, the application of what is learned is limited, and the measurement of its *effectives* is limited. We have learned the following: For leadership development to be effective, organizations must first fix their operating system and then train leaders on the new operating system. If you don't, then leaders return from trainings on Monday morning into the same context that they cannot change themselves. This is why systems need to be fixed before leadership.

The road map is a transformation programme with initiatives that address specific key issues and gaps. These initiatives range from self-study, organizational, managerial, design, and operating initiatives to education, training, and mentoring. The right combination of measures makes a transformation succeed.

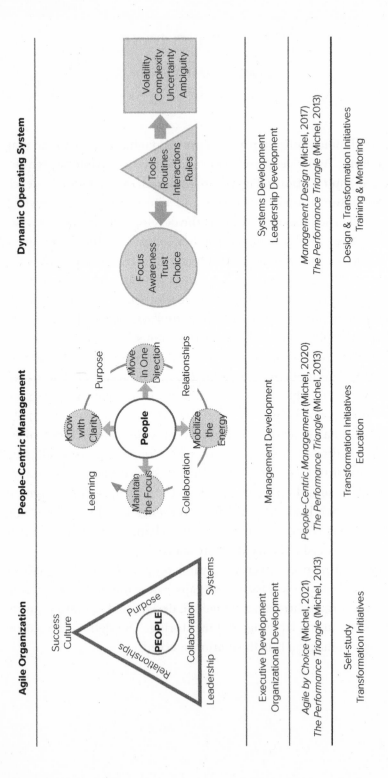

FIGURE 56: THE DEVELOPMENT PROGRAMME

AGILE

The Performance Triangle frames the capabilities of an agile organization. Figure 57 represents the essential capabilities of an organization's operating system. It summarizes the people, organization, and work elements.

Elements	Learning Opportunities
People: The inner game with focus, awareness, choice, and trust	Practise the exercises with Nudges 3–6 from *Agile by Choice* (Michel, 2021)
Resources: time, attention, energy, space	Be aware of your return on management
	Practise the exercises with Nudges 7–11 from *Agile by Choice* (Michel, 2021
Capabilities: motivation, experience, knowledge, skills	Practise the exercises with Nudge 12 from *Agile by Choice* (Michel, 2021)
Organization: systems, leadership, and culture	Practise the exercises with Nudge 2 from *Agile by Choice* (Michel, 2021)
	Use the definitions, practices, insights, and literature cited in *The Performance Triangle* (Michel, 2013)
	Retrieve sources and resources from the Knowledge Hub at management-insights.ch
Work: purpose, relationships, and collaboration	Practise the exercises with Nudge 2 from *Agile by Choice* (Michel, 2021)
	Use the definitions, practices, insights, and literature cited in *The Performance Triangle* (Michel, 2013)
	Retrieve sources and resources from the Knowledge Hub at management-insights.ch

FIGURE 57: AGILE DEVELOPMENT

The inner-game technique comes naturally to people. But few are aware of their capabilities because they've lost the natural proficiency they had as children. Moreover, executives who've been accustomed to the control mode cannot imagine what the inner game can do for them and their teams. That's why we created the exercises in *Agile by Choice* (Michel, 2021) – to help leaders gain that personal experience of the inner game.

Return on management is a conceptual formula to measure how effectively we use our resources. Similar to the inner game, the practice of time, attention, energy, and space requires experience and grows with its use. To get started, *Agile by Choice* offers another set of exercises.

In *The Performance Triangle*, we extensively documented the purpose, definitions, practices, insights, and literature on the agile features of systems, leadership, culture, purpose, relationships, and collaboration. With this, engaging executives in the diagnostic and the team workshop is the best development opportunity. Their own insights are the best motivation for successful change.

PEOPLE-CENTRIC

Four principles, the Leadership Scorecard, and the dominant leadership style determine people-centric management. Figure 58 presents learning and development opportunities for management.

Elements	Learning Opportunities
Principles: Self-responsibility, delegation, self-organization, focus of attention	Practise the exercises with Nudges 1–6 from *Agile by Choice* (Michel, 2021) Define and implement transformation initiatives in line with four shifts based on *People-Centric Management* (Michel, 2020)
Leadership Scorecard: 20 culture, leadership and systems elements	Use the definitions, practices, insights, and literature cited in *The Performance Triangle* (Michel, 2013) Educate leaders on the people-centric scorecard
Leadership style	Train leaders on the dominant leadership style

FIGURE 58: PEOPLE-CENTRIC DEVELOPMENT

Altering managerial principles is a deep intervention. As such, it requires a carefully selected set of development and education initiatives. Moreover, Better Management isn't a quick fix to add to your existing way of running a business. It's a fundamental change in every principle, process, and practice. And while early successes will quickly materialize, it takes years of hard work to complete the transformation.

The Leadership Scorecard spells out the key capabilities needed for that transformation. The Performance Triangle offers the details of these capabilities in 20 elements. Embedding these capabilities into the organization takes education. Changing behaviour and the decision-making approach is hard, as old patterns dominate everything we do. And so, it takes training and persistence for a new leadership style to evolve.

DYNAMIC

The Leadership Toolbox adds dynamic features to the operating system. Figure 59 introduces learning and development opportunities for management.

Elements	Learning Opportunities
Leadership Toolbox: 20 elements as rules, routines, interactions, and tools	Learn about diagnostic mentoring to decide on your dominant management context, the operating model, and the principles to determine the design of your Leadership Toolbox. Use the definitions, practices, insights, and literature from *The Performance Triangle* (Michel, 2013).
	Purpose: Identify the toolbox that fits the operating model.
	Features: Close the gaps in your existing toolbox.
	Choice: Select the elements that meet the needs of your organization's demographics.
	Develop and implement systems through specific transformation initiatives.
	Train and counsel leaders in the use of systems through dedicated leadership development programmes.

FIGURE 59: DYNAMIC DEVELOPMENT

Systems are the primary intervention point for change in people's behaviours, decision-making, and actions in organizations. The Leadership Toolbox is the most effective lever to address a dynamic context. The design of a toolbox with dynamic features is the most important intervention in any organization. This is why the development and implementation of a new toolbox requires special care.

A large part of diagnostic mentoring is dedicated to the design of the toolbox with dynamic features. While design is an expert task, leaders need to understand how to use the toolbox to their own benefit. The design, development, and implementation of a new Leadership Toolbox follows specific transformation initiatives. While change in the toolbox is a comparably easy intervention, it does not just happen by itself.

The toolbox is the means to scale management across an entire organization. A poorly stocked toolbox has long legs. It infiltrates all parts of an organization. This is why the design of the toolbox is expert work and requires the CEO's attention. With a dynamic toolbox, businesses have the capabilities to scale management.

Equally important is the training and mentoring of leaders in the use of the new Leadership Toolbox. This is important, because a dynamic toolbox is fundamentally different from a traditional toolbox. Such training must be part of the road map.

With the following questions, initiate your development work.
- Have you identified the development activities for agile, people-centric and dynamic capabilities?

If your answer is no, what can you do?
- Engage your experts to help you with this step.
- Consider diagnostic mentoring for experienced experts.

With the following, Part V, we change from design and development to Better Management: Work *in* the System.

INITIATE THE DEVELOPMENT

The road map provides a set of initiatives to develop agile, people-centric, and dynamic capabilities. Initiate the development offers guidance and ideas to turn the programme into a development manual.

KEY CHAPTER IDEAS

- Developing agile, people-centric, and dynamic capabilities combines dedicated initiatives, education, design, training, and mentoring

ACTION AGENDA

- Complement your road map plan with the development of details and turn it into a transformation manual.

FURTHER READING

Michel, L (2021). *Diagnostic Mentoring: How to Transform the Way We Manage.* London: LID Publishing.

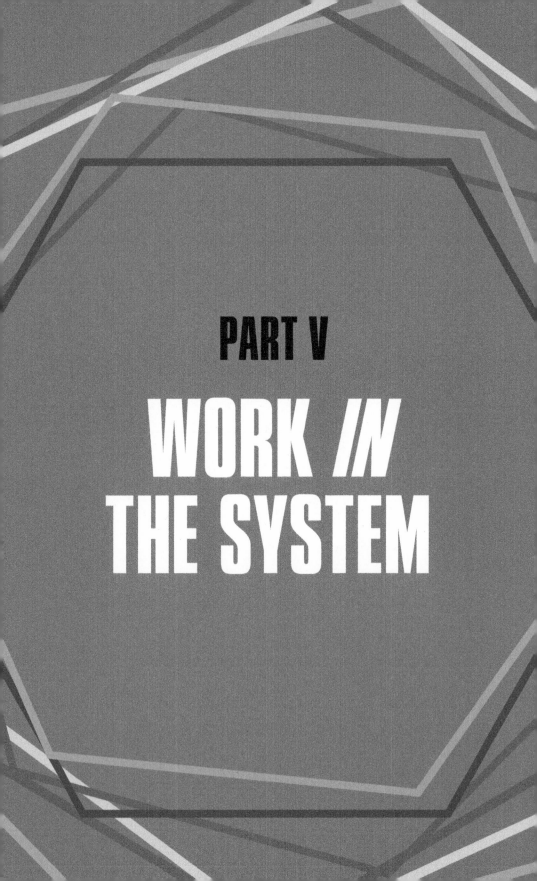

PART V

WORK *IN* THE SYSTEM

People first is an important principle for Better Management. Work *in* the system is the prerequisite for distributed leadership and brings clarity, direction, energy, and focus to the entire organization. The shift to Better Management initiates with top management.

SET THE RIGHT PRIORITIES

As a manager, it is important to be clear about your priorities: people first, organization second, clients third, and owner forth. Getting these priorities right is an important step toward Better Management.

PRIORITIES

The shift to Better Management starts by setting priorities right. The Performance Triangle helps you establish people-centric, agile, and dynamic capabilities at scale, with the right priorities in mind (Figure 60).

Peter Drucker provided the guidance for management: "There is only one valid purpose of a corporation: to create a customer." Drucker saw that a company's primary responsibility is to create value for customers. With that purpose in mind, the question then comes about where managers set their priorities. I am quite clear: it's people who serve clients. That's why the priority for managers becomes: people first (they are in the centre); agile second (the organization); client-focused third (the work environment); and dynamic operations fourth (your responsibility as a manager).

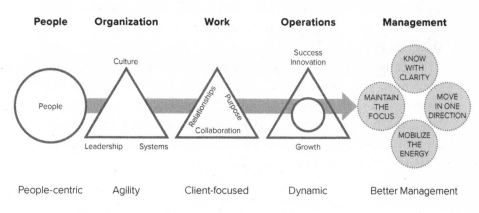

FIGURE 60: THE RIGHT PRIORITIES

Better Managers establish an environment aligned with four priorities, so keep this in mind while you work on the system, which is your primary responsibility:

1. People are the centre of your attention: People-centric demands an individualized environment where people can unlock their talent and perform at their peak. It's people who deliver value to clients.

They should be able to experience flow, the state where challenges and capabilities meet to create a positive experience. That's the ultimate goal of people-centric management. As a leader, it is your task (and your obligation) to create that kind of work environment.

2. Your organization sets the context: Agile capabilities enable people-centric management. Systems, leadership, and culture establish the operating environment for people to apply their talent and perform. Hence, it is important to be clear about the potential and interference in your own organization.

3. It's people who work who care about clients: People-centric and agile principles enable you as a leader to demand self-responsibility, delegate work, facilitate self-organization, and lead with broad directives. This means that the people in your organization can take charge and take care of clients. Client focus is all about your people making sure that valuable clients are satisfied, come back, and want more.

4. Success is what appeals to owners: They look for growth and return on their investment. Growth comes from clients who come back. Operational returns come from capabilities, efficiency gains, and innovations. Long-term value creation must be the goal of the business.

Getting these priorities right balances the interests of all stakeholders in your business. It creates public value (Meynhardt and Gomez, 2013). People-centric management based on agile capabilities and a dynamic operating system creates value for society, regardless of whether you operate in a traditional or a dynamic mode.

Better Management assumes that you put people first.

What about your priorities?
- Have you decided on your managerial priorities?

If your answer is no, what can you do?
- Engage your team into the discussion.

The following, Chapter 22, makes the case to establish leadership everywhere based on Better Management.

SET THE RIGHT PRIORITIES

Better Management is clear about managerial priorities: People first, organization second, client-focus third, and dynamic operations with success for owners fourth. In combination, this makes Better Management every manager's job.

KEY CHAPTER IDEAS

- People are the centre of your attention.
- Your organization sets the context.
- It's people who work who care about clients.
- Success is what appeals to owners.

ACTION AGENDA

- Getting these priorities right is an important step toward Better Management.

FURTHER READING

Michel, L (2020). *People-Centric Management: How Managers Use Four Levers to Bring Out the Greatness of Others.* London: LID Publishing.

CHAPTER

22

LEADERSHIP IS EVERYWHERE

Better Management is work *in* the system with four principles: Clarity, direction, energy, and focus. Well developed, this establishes leadership everywhere. The responsibility for Better Management is with the individual and the institution. It's all about keeping people in mind.

WORK *IN* THE SYSTEM

Work *in* the system is Better Management. Business is about identifying, selecting, and transforming opportunities into value. With the people in mind, managers can now use four principles as their means to deliver value with their teams in a dynamic environment. Better Managers apply the following principles with their teams (Figure 61):

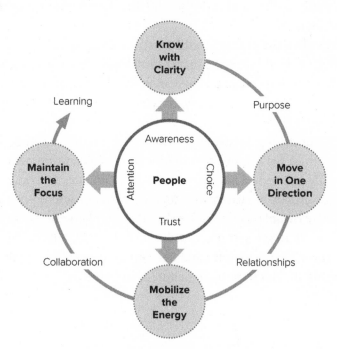

FIGURE 61: WORK *IN* THE SYSTEM

1. Know with clarity: Raise awareness. Help people find purpose. They know that motivation stems from self-responsibility. Purpose replaces incentives. All managers need to do for people is help them make sense of what truly matters. That's the best way to identify opportunities and deal with the complexity in your business.

2. Move in one direction: Enable choice. Relate with people to enhance knowledge. Better managers delegate decisions and relate with people to enhance their skills and knowledge. Choice and direction are their means to bundle the energy, help them select the right opportunities, and move in one direction as their way to deal with ambiguity.

3. Mobilize the energy: Build trust. Facilitate collaboration. Better managers facilitate self-organization based on trust as the means to deal with uncertainty. They mobilize resources in ways that enable collaboration across organizational boundaries, which turns opportunities into value.

4. Maintain the focus: Focus attention. Enable learning. Better managers use beliefs and boundaries to keep attention centred on what truly matters. They know that focus enables learning as the means to unlock creativity and to stick with chosen opportunities, despite the turbulence of higher volatility. Applying Better Management is work *in* the system. You should expect all your managers to follow these four principles and develop their enabling approach to management, which caters to people as individuals.

LEADERSHIP
EVERYWHERE

Better Management means leadership everywhere (Figure 62). Clients offer the purpose, and the organization sets the context. That's why raising awareness for speed, agile capabilities and resilience touches everyone in organizations.

It is increasingly recognized that companies need to be fast, agile, and resilient. Speed represents the ability to implement strategy quickly. Agility provides the capacity to consistently change without having to change. Resilience adds stability, as the capability to absorb, react to, and potentially reinvent the business model. Speed, agility, and resilience represent dynamic capabilities. Their purpose is to enable the organization to reconfigure its resources to quickly adapt to a changing environment.

The inner game is the technique that every individual applies to become agile. Individual agility allows managers to delegate decisions to the client front, which speeds up decision-making. As a result, the CEO and the board will appreciate peak performance everywhere.

A shared culture, interactive leadership, and dynamic systems are the elements that enable organizational agility. It's everyone's task to work on the system and make the organization agile. It certainly is every manager's primary job. As a result, the business has what it takes to become a truly innovative organization. In return, the CEO and the board have a chance to make innovation part of their strategy.

Everyone needs to care about purpose, collaboration, and relationships. Together, this will make organizations more resilient. As a result, growth becomes part of the strategy.

Performance, innovation, and growth are the scoreboard for the CEO and the board. It's their responsibility to ensure that everyone assumes leadership, with a focus on outcomes.

Focus	People	Organization	Work	Operations
Everyone	Inner Game	Culture Leadership Systems	Purpose Collaboration Relationships	Operating Environment
Managers	Speed	Agility	Resilience	Dynamic Capabilities
CEO and Board	Performance	Innovation	Growth	Outcomes

FIGURE 62: LEADERSHIP EVERYWHERE

The purpose of a company is to create a customer. It's people who make it happen. Autonomy and decentralization push responsibility to where the work takes place. As such, self-organizing teams make decisions. With this, decisions are made, timely and with the expertise of the right people. This means delegated leadership to quickly respond to client needs. That means leadership is everywhere.

Raising awareness for agile is everyone's task. Better Management helps you and everyone in your organization turn your management into a competitive advantage.

WHO IS
RESPONSIBLE?

The shift to Better Management, whether it's a disruption or an evolution, is about learning. The question becomes one of who's responsible for making the shift in the operating system happen.

Learning has three roles: readiness, capabilities, and opportunity. Readiness rests with the individual. Learning is an individual accountability. It requires awareness, focus, trust, and choice. Capability is a shared responsibility between people and the institution. Leaders need to provide the opportunity. Then, it's up to the individual to capture that opportunity. Opportunity resides with the institution. It is the institution's role to provide the opportunity. As such, institutions and individuals have different roles and accountabilities to make the shift to Better Management.

But, without exception, any decision to pursue a transformation lies with top management. It fundamentally alters the DNA of the organization. It assumes self-responsibility, which is an altogether different image of mankind. Decisions are delegated to the client front. Networks of teams organize themselves. And broad objectives inspire people and maintain their focus. Systems, leadership, and culture are at stake.

At the same time, this dramatic change alters the role of leaders. It's their task to establish a work environment where people can unlock their full talent. And leaders control through interaction – their onsite presence and support for people to get work done.

The transformation to Better Management alters the functioning of an entire organization. When team- or department-level change projects without the consent to alter systems, leadership and culture are doomed to fail.

KEEP THE PEOPLE
IN MIND

The clues to performance are potential and interference. Interference limits the potential. With this, the question is what learning and development need to focus on: the potential or sources of interference. Purpose, inner-game techniques, resources, and capabilities must be part of every road map development programme.

The overall goal of Better Management is to help leaders create an operating environment where people can unlock their full talent. Agile organizations, people-centric management, and dynamic capabilities are features that do both: unlock the potential and limit interference. Figure 63 introduces the concept, with a focus on what people need to perform at their peak.

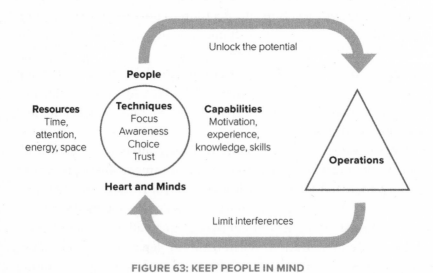

FIGURE 63: KEEP PEOPLE IN MIND

People come with potential, their heart, inner-game techniques, resources, and capabilities. Operations offer the playing field. With this comes the commitment to support the development. And they offer the ability to find purpose – the condition that allows people to be part of the organization, from their hearts to their heads.

The operating system with strategy, vision, values and a workplace where employees connect and build relationships helps to engage people's **hearts and minds**. Purpose is not a given. It needs to be developed and constantly nurtured. As such, it must be part of every road map and at the heart of any development initiative.

Inner-game **techniques** with awareness, choice, trust, and focus offer a route to purpose, which helps people learn and perform at their peak. The purpose is to limit the self-made interfering effects – the doubts, stress, fear, bias, limiting concepts, and assumptions. With this, people are able to access their capabilities and resources. The ideal is leadership and systems with a design that fits and limits interference. Better management is not a given. It needs to be constantly reinforced as part of an ongoing process of training and development.

Resources are limited. Time that has passed cannot be recovered. Focus that is lost needs to be regained. Energy needs constant refuelling. And space is limited relative to time – one can only be at one place in time. Managing one's own resources is demanding. Managers who care about a healthy work environment pay attention to how people manage their own resources. Research is quite clear about the benefits of a healthy work environment. Management's own resources must be part of every development initiative.

Capabilities such as motivation, experience, knowledge, and skills are often taken for granted – "That's what we hire people for." Some call it talent. We have extensively discussed motivation: it comes with self-responsibility. Leaders can only demotivate. Any attempt to motivate self-responsible people has the opposite effect: demotivation. Experience comes with its use. Hence, exposing people to new experiences is development. Knowledge grows with use. In an enabling operating environment, people apply and grow their knowledge for the benefit of the organization. Most skills are context-specific. Applying them in other contexts may require additional training. It is important to note that most capabilities must be constantly applied to keep them at the expected level. Development is one of the means to keep capabilities ready to be used.

What about your management?
- Does your management follow the principles of Better Management?
- Is Better Management the standard throughout your organization?

If your answers are no, what can you do?
- Better Management requires practice. Work at it.
- Train your managers in Better Management.

The following, Chapter 23, claims that people are the ends.

LEADERSHIP IS EVERYWHERE

Work *in* the system refers to the daily operation of Better Management. Clarity, direction, energy, and focus are the levers to establish leadership everywhere.

KEY CHAPTER IDEAS

- Work in the system is the daily work of a better manager.
- Better Management establishes leadership everywhere.
- The responsibility is with the individual and the institution.
- With a change in the operating system, keep people in mind.

ACTION AGENDA

- Train and practice Better Management throughout your organization.

FURTHER READING

Michel, L (2021). *Agile by Choice: How You Can Make the Shift to Establish Leadership Everywhere*. London: LID Publishing.

Michel, L (2020). *People-Centric Management: How Managers Use Four Levers to Bring Out the Greatness of Others*. London: LID Publishing.

PEOPLE ARE THE ENDS

The shift to Better Management starts with a mind shift but with an experience that most leaders don't have. Once it reaches the tipping point, Better Management releases productive energy. It's a learning journey for your entire team to simultaneously work *on* and *in* the system. The destination is Better Management as your competitive advantage with people as the ends.

A MIND SHIFT

The shift to Better Management first and foremost requires a mind shift from heroic leadership to leadership everywhere with collective minds (Figure 64) that serve the company's main purpose: to create a customer. The shift fundamentally alters our work environment and how we perform and use resources and requires a toolbox that is designed around people making decisions.

In a people-centric organization, the work environment shifts from delivering tangible outcomes to applying knowledge to create intangible products. People apply the inner game to cope with the challenges of the outer game and therefore act on their own. They rely on their own resources to get work done. The focus shifts from power to unlocking talents. And the dynamic toolbox supports delegated decision-making.

	From traditional ...	... to Better Management
Work environment (outer game)	Stable, transactions, tangible, remote	Dynamic, knowledge, intangible, in touch with customers
Performance (inner game)	Plan, do, check, act	Awareness, choice, trust
Resources	Power	Energy, focus of attention, time, space, accountability
Toolbox	Hierarchy, separation of thinking and doing	Dynamic tools and decision-making

FIGURE 64: A MIND SHIFT

For most executives, the shift to Better Management and the choice of people-centric and dynamic capabilities are not part of their experience. They have been domesticated in a context that has always required traditional and tangible forms of control, power, and hierarchy.

A TIPPING POINT

Management as a true competitive advantage may require unlocking industry boundaries to find your own best approach. This will require developmental energy until it releases productive energies. The shift to people-centricity, agility, and dynamic capabilities does not come for free. For most of us, traditional ways of doing things are known and deeply anchored in our habits. Overcoming our habits and leaving behind things that have worked in the past requires energy. However, from many successful transformations, my organization has observed that the investment in attention and time reaches a tipping point (Figure 65) where the energy becomes productive, and the results become visible.

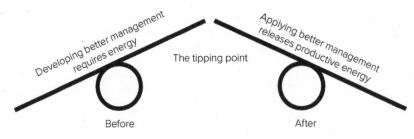

FIGURE 65: A TIPPING POINT

The tipping point is one of those defining moments when flow occurs and the return to traditional is no longer an option. Leaders who have 'crossed the Rubicon' to Better Management explain that energy flows, they've recovered time for important things, and their focus of attention enables them to continuously learn and adapt.

IT'S A LEARNING JOURNEY

Diagnostic mentoring creates the learning experience you need to successfully transform to Better Management. Awareness, insights, and learning guide your journey, with the tools to engage your team (Figure 66).

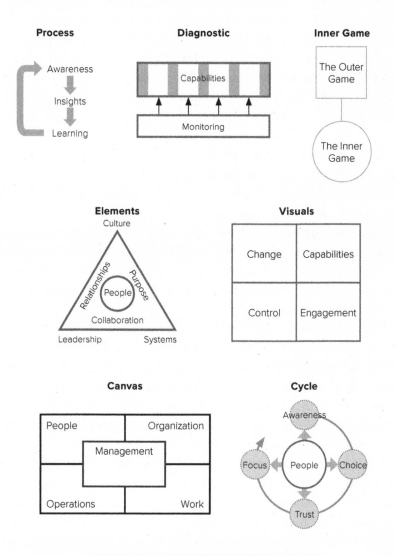

FIGURE 66: DIAGNOSTIC MENTORING TOOLS

Raise awareness: The diagnostic establishes observation points. Monitoring is a discipline that can be used to observe and alter design. By observing (scanning) capabilities, potential faults, and malfunctions can be spotted at an early stage. By becoming aware of critical signals, potential design requirements can be identified. In this way, leaders can decide whether or not to address issues. As such, monitoring initiates design changes relating to capabilities.

Act on your insights: The Performance Triangle distils the elements of Better Management. The use of agile, people-centric, and dynamic capabilities, and design, is selective. The decision to employ a specific design excludes other alternatives. The design process is about the selection of managerial tools, routines, and rules that make for Better Management. Design requires reflection and interactions. It is not free from politics. The setting of these conversations determines much about the design's quality.

Expedite the learning: The inner game offers the techniques for learning. Monitoring assumes that the design is reversible and not frozen in place. While deeply embedded in organizational practices and rooted in the past, managerial design and capabilities can be changed through interventions. The shift to Better Management guides specific capability development projects in line with decisions on what needs to be changed. In this way, the idea of permanent change is replaced by the notion of combining learning and doing. It is an iterative process.

The agile, people-centric, and dynamic capabilities transformation starts with the personal shift every leader needs to make. Self-responsibility, delegation, self-organization, and focus of attention are principles that aren't part of the experience of most leaders. It takes experience to make the shift. This is why I suggest that leaders first work through *Agile by Choice*, the book that offers gentle nudges for the shift.

The traditional negative assumptions about people, and the dominant Cartesian mindset, are the main obstacles to any transformation. Success means applying the same people-centric, agile, and dynamic principles to the transformation as it does to Better Management. It builds on the humanistic tradition in Europe. Readers can find the details in *People-Centric Management*, the book that serves as a model to Better Management.

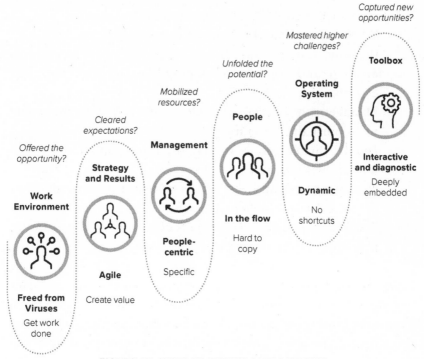

FIGURE 67: STEPS TO BETTER MANAGEMENT

Better is the standard that qualifies management as a competitive advantage. The standard comes in steps (Figure 67) that are increasingly demanding, have greater impact and offer higher sustainability:

- A viruses-free, collaborative, connected, and purposeful work environment for people to *get work done.*
- A strategy with agile capabilities that safeguards performance, innovation, and growth for the organization to be successful and *create value.*
- People-centric management with principles for self-responsible people who make the client offering *specific.*
- People who play the inner game to experience flow, which makes performance *hard to copy.*
- An operating system with dynamic principles that allows *no short cuts.*
- A toolbox with diagnostic systems for interactive leadership that is *deeply embedded in culture.*

What can you do to reach the better standards?

- **Work environment**: Remove the interference and offer the opportunity.
- **Strategy and results**: Develop agile capabilities and clear expectations.
- **Management**: Engage in people-centric principles for people to mobilize their resources.
- **People**: Enable people to play the inner game for them to unfold their potential.
- **Operating System**: Insist on dynamic features in support of people to master higher challenges.
- **Toolbox**: Maintain a diagnostic toolbox for people to capture new opportunities and grow.

Every executive, organization, and operating system is unique. That's why diagnostic mentoring uses a diagnostic to monitor capabilities, applies the inner-game techniques for expedited learning, uses visual thinking aids to offer options, facilitates conversations with the canvas and guides management with the people-centric cycle. It's the process that uses experience, suggests principles and guides the transformation to Better Management. Better Management means leadership everywhere. It's a team process that simultaneously works *on* the system while people work *in* the system.

DOES BETTER
MAKE A DIFFERENCE?

So far, we have introduced the features of Better Management and the steps to get there. Does it matter?

To find out, in Figure 68 we compare the scores of top-tier organizations that have adopted Better Management with those that come with traditional management. The evidence is clear: in all areas that make up a competitive advantage, Better Management yields significantly better scores.

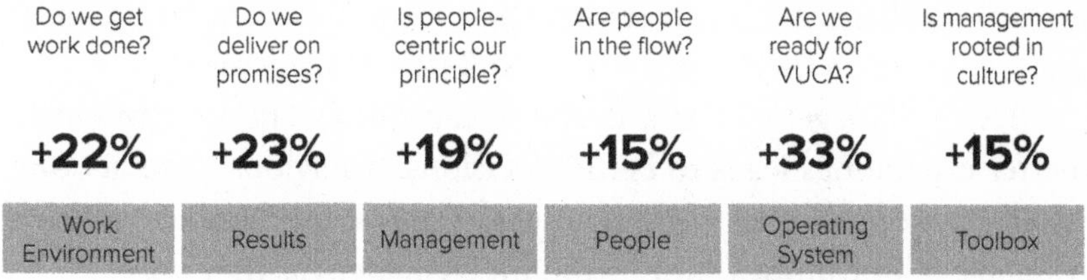

Do we get work done?	Do we deliver on promises?	Is people-centric our principle?	Are people in the flow?	Are we ready for VUCA?	Is management rooted in culture?
+22%	**+23%**	**+19%**	**+15%**	**+33%**	**+15%**
Work Environment	Results	Management	People	Operating System	Toolbox

Scores of top-tier organizations that have adopted better management vs. middle tier organizations.

FIGURE 68: DOES BETTER MAKE A DIFFERERENCE?

Overall, better-managed organizations make a difference. They are considerably more agile, people-centric, and ready for a dynamic market environment. And they are better off competing in the future: performance is 21% higher, innovation 25% higher, and growth 28% higher.

Better management increases intangible value. The responsiveness to customer needs is up by 17%, alignment +16%, capabilities +18%, employee motivation +15% and cleverness +20%.

Better Management is a yardstick. Investments in Better Management clearly pay off.

THE BETTER WAY

Better Management is needed to operate in the new dynamic business context. Diagnostic mentoring is the better way to transform how we lead people, organize work, and perform in that dynamic environment.

Diagnostic mentoring combines mentoring, diagnostics, design thinking, and experiential learning, with the goal being to develop agile organizations, people-centric management, and dynamic operating systems with teams. The journey starts with the leader, who personally makes the shift to people-centricity. Agile establishes the necessary work environment for people to unlock their talents. The dynamic operating system enables businesses to operate in the context. With this, leaders can engage their teams in diagnostic mentoring to transform their organization to Better Management.

Better Management is a dynamic capability. The investment in better capabilities leads to better decisions, behaviours, and actions. With it, people unlock their potential, remove interference, capture valuable opportunities, and surmount challenges as they arise.

Better Management is every manager's primary job. Diagnostic mentoring is the social technology that offers the observation points to create awareness, intervention points for the call to action, and leverage points for expedited learning. It comes with a process, a diagnostic, the inner-game mental technique, 50+ elements, 30 visuals, the canvas facilitation tool and a mentoring cycle. It's the better way for managers to remove outdated management practices by creating awareness, action on insights, and expedited learning.

Early signs are promising, as I see the new practice inform new theories used in business schools to train future leaders in Better Management. It's exciting to learn that the initial set of classes were deemed a success, conveying stuff that truly matters to managers, and that the first MBA schoolbook on diagnostic mentoring is about to be published.

Better Management is every manager's primary job. Now it's your turn to engage in diagnostic mentoring and transform your management into a competitive advantage. Do it with your people in mind.

PEOPLE ARE THE ENDS

For most leaders, engaging in Better Management means a mind shift from control to enabling. And it requires an experience that most don't have. That's why the development of Better Management requires energy. Once the tipping point is achieved, it all comes back with lots of energy. Better Management is the destination and the competitive advantage.

KEY CHAPTER IDEAS

- The shift from traditional to Better Management requires a mind shift.
- Once the tipping point is reached, there is no return to traditional. The energy for Better Management is huge.
- Diagnostic mentoring is the methodology to develop Better Management.
- The better way is when people are part of it.

ACTION AGENDA

- It's time to start you own journey to Better Management.

FURTHER READING

Michel, L (2021). *Diagnostic Mentoring: How to Transform the Way We Manage*. London: LID Publishing.

APPENDIX:
THE BETTER MANAGEMENT NOTE PAD

Part I: Map your challenges

 Work
Environment

 Strategy
and Results

 Management

Part II: Review the six principles

Offered the opportunity?   *Cleared expectations?*   *Mobilized resources?*

Part III: Design better management

Freed from viruses?   *Agile?*   *People-centric?*

Part IV: Develop the capabilities

Get work done?   Deliver on promises?   Unique value proposition?
Create value?   Specific?

Part V: Work in the system

My work environment?   My strategy?   My management?
My results?

People   **Operating System**   **Toolbox**

Unfolded the potential?   *Mastered higher challenges?*   *Captured new opportunities?*

In the flow?   Dynamic?   Interactive and diagnostic?

Exceed expectations?   Ready for VUCA?   Deeply embedded
Hard to copy?   No shortcuts   in culture?

My performance?   My operations?   My leadership and systems?

BIBLIOGRAPHY

Aghina, W, Handscomb, C, Salo, O, & Thaker, S (2021). The Impact on Agility: How to Shape Your Organization to Compete. *MyKinsey Insights*, https://www.mckinsey.com/business-functions/people-and-organizational-performance/our-insights/the-impact-of-agility-how-to-shape-your-organization-to-compete, last retrieved on 9 January 2022.

Ansoff, H (1980). Strategic issue management. *Strategic Management Journal*, 1, 131-148.

Bäcklander, G (2019). Doing Complexity Leadership Theory: How Agile Coaches at Spotify Practice Enabling Leadership. *Creativity and Innovation Management*, 28:42-60.

Barney, JB (1991). Firm Resources and Sustained Competitive Advantage. *Journal of Management*, 17(1): 99-120.

Beer, M, Finnström, M; and Schrader, D (2016). Why Leadership Training Fails – And What to Do About It. *Harvard Business Review*. June 2016.

Christensen, CM (2015). *The Innovator's Dilemma: When New Technologies Cause Great Firms to Fail*. Boston, Massachusetts: Harvard Business Review Press.

Crocitto, M & Youssef, M (2003). The Human Side of Organizational Agility. *Industrial Management and Data Systems*, 103,338-397.

Csikszentmihalyi, M (1990). *The Psychology of the Optimal Experience*. New York: Harper & Row.

Denning, S (2021). What the Key Management Problem is Often at the Top. *Forbes*: https://www.forbes.com/sites/stevedenning/2021/11/07/why-the-key-management-problem-is-often-at-the-top, last retrieved 9 January 2022.

Drucker, PF (1992). The New Society of Organizations. *Harvard Business Review*, September-October 1992.

Drucker, PF (2006). *The Effective Executive: The Definitive Guide to Getting the Right Things Done*. New York: Harper Business Essentials.

Dunning, D (2011). The Dunning–Kruger Effect: On Being Ignorant of One's Own Ignorance. 44. *Advances in Experimental Social Psychology*: 247–296.

Edmondson, A (2018). *The Fearless Organization: Creating Psychological Safety in the Workplace for Learning, Innovation, and Growth*. Hoboken, New Jersey: Wiley.

Gallwey, WT (2000). *The Inner Game of Work*. New York: Random House.

Glaveski, S (2019). Where Companies Go Wrong with Learning and Development. *Harvard Business Review*, October 2019.

Ghoshal, S (2005). Bad Management Theories Are Destroying Good Management Practices. *Academy of Management Learning & Education*. Vol. 4, No. 1. Pages 75-91.

Greiner, LE (1997). Evolution and Revolution as Organizations Grow: A Company's Past Has Clues for Management That Are Critical to Future Success. *Family Business Review*, 10(4), 397–409.

Habermas, J (1988). *Moralbewusstsein und kommunikatives Handeln*. 3. Aufl. Frankfurt a M.

Hagel, J (2021). Is Digital Transformation Missing the Real Opportunity? https://www.johnhagel.com/is-digital-transformation-missing-the-real-opportunity/, last retrieved 10 January 2022.

Hax, AC and Majluf, ND (1996). *The Strategy Concept and Process: A Pragmatic Approach*. New York: Palgrave.

Hill, A (2021). How Management Fashions Can Change the World. Financial Times: https://www.ft.com/content/f14b3205-f140-4e74-8743-04b881b63134, last retrieved 9 January 2022.

Hugos, MH (2013). *Business Agility: Sustainable Prosperity in a Relentlessly Competitive World*. Hoboken, New Jersey, John Wiley and Sons.

Kahneman, D (2011). *Thinking, Fast and Slow*. USA: Macmillan.

Lang, D & Rumsey, C (2018). Business Disruption Is Here to Stay – What Should Leaders Do? *Quality – Access to Success*, 19(35-40).

Lawrence, PR & Lorsch JW (1967). *Organization and Environment: Managing Differentiation and Integration*. Boston, Massachusetts: Harvard Business School Press.

Luhmann, N (1995). *Social Systems*. Stanford: Stanford University Press.

McKinsey (2017). How to Create an Agile Organization. Survey report.

Meynhardt, T & Gomez, P (2013). Organisationen schöpfen Wert für die Gesellschaft. In: Heuser, J et al. *DIE ZEIT erklärt die Wirtschaft* (199–207). Hamburg: Murmann.

Michel, L (2013). *The Performance Triangle: Diagnostic Mentoring to Manage Organizations and People for Superior Performance in Turbulent Times*. London: LID Publishing.

Michel, L (2020). *People-Centric Management: How Managers Use Four Levers to Bring Out the Greatness of Others*. London: LID Publishing.

Michel, L (2021). *Diagnostic Mentoring: How to Transform the Way We Manage*. London: LID Publishing.

Michel, L (2021). *Management Design: Managing People and Organizations in Turbulent Times* (Third ed.). London: LID Publishing.

Michel, L (2021). *Agile by Choice: How You Can Make the Shift to Establish Leadership Everywhere*. London: LID Publishing.

Michel, L, Anzengruber, J, Wolfe, M, & Hixson, N (2018). Under What Conditions Do Rules-Based and Capabilities-Based Management Modes Dominate? Special Issue *Risks in Financial and Real Estate Markets Journal*, 6(32).

Murray, A & Greenes, K (2006). New Leadership Strategies for the Entreprise of the Future. *VINE*, 36:358-370.

Nold, H, Anzengruber, J, Michel, L, & Wolfle, M (2018). Organizational Agility: Testing Validity and Reliability of a Diagnostic Instrument. *Journal of Organizational Psychology*, 18(3).

Nold, H & Michel, L (2016). The Performance Triangle: A Model for Corporate Agility. *Leadership & Organizational Development Journal*, 37(3).

Porter, M (1985). *Competitive Advantage: Creating and Sustaining Superior Performance*. New York: Free Press.

Salmador, M & Bueno, E (2007). Knowledge Creation in Strategy-Making: Implications for Theory and Practice. *European Journal of Innovation Management*, 10:367-390.

Scholtes, PR (1998). *The Leader'. Handbook. Making Things Happen. Getting Things Done*. New York: McGraw-Hill.

Senge, PM (1990). *The Fifth Discipline*, New York: Doubleday.

Simons, R (1995). *Levers Of Control: How Managers Use Innovative Control Systems to Drive Strategic Renewal*. Boston: Harvard Business School Press.

Sull, D, Homkes R & Sull, C (2015). Why Strategy Implementation Unravels – and What To Do About It. *Harvard Business Review*, March 2015.

Sutton, Robert I (2014). Eight Essentials for Scaling Up Without Screwing Up. *Harvard Business Review*, February.

von Foerster, H (1992). *Observing Systems*. Seaside, CA: Intersystems Publication.

LIST OF FIGURES

ACKNOWLEDGEMENTS

The idea for *Better Management* initiated with the foundation of Management Insights AG and the initiation of our diagnostic mentoring community 20 years ago. Its mission is to change the world through Better Management.

It took some years from the idea to finally publishing the new book. We first had to work on some of the foundations, such as *The Performance Triangle, People-Centric Management,* and *Diagnostic Mentoring* to establish the models required for *Better Management*. Our research team published the critical papers on our models and the diagnostic, the members of our community used the insights with their clients, and many clients used the diagnostic reports with the models and the methodology to work on Better Management. The benefit of waiting now is that Better Management has hardened. Its underlying foundation is anchored in science and the result has been proven in practice.

As such, I am thankful to our research team, to the many clients and to the members of our community. Professor Herb Nold from Polk State College in Lakeland, Florida and Professor Johanna Anzengruber from the University of Applied Sciences of Upper Austria in Linz, Austria, have worked hard to get the Performance Triangle, the diagnostic and context framework published. Thank you to both of you for our friendship over the past many years and your engagement for our shared cause, Better Management.

Executives from 400 companies have used our diagnostic tool that underpins Better Management. Many of them have engaged in the diagnostic mentoring methodology to work on becoming people-centric, agile, and dynamic organizations. Thank you to every client that has contributed to making *Better Management* happen.

My thanks also go to the 40 members of our community who have used the diagnostic and applied the models as part of their work with clients. With your feedback, you have all helped me refine the model and the software behind the diagnostic reporting that connect Better Management with diagnostic mentoring.

Finally, my utmost thanks go to my wife, Charleen. I have been hiding behind my Mac, writing and programming for too long. I am very thankful for her support.

Lukas Michel
St Moritz, Switzerland
February 2022

ABOUT THE AUTHOR

Lukas Michel is the owner of Management Insights AG, based in Switzerland, with its global network of experienced business mentors.

In addition to lecturing at universities, licensing his own agile mentoring methodology, writing on management issues and building his consulting network, Lukas is a business leader with a track record of balance sheet accountability in his work for global corporations in Europe and Asia.

Over the course of his 40-year career, he has worked with executive teams around the world, focusing on management and agility in a diverse range of local, national, and global organizations.

For the last 20 years, Lukas has been developing diagnostic mentoring, the methodology that offers diagnostics and a common framework and language for scaling 'agile' capabilities across all organizational levels.

He holds an MS degree in management from North Carolina State University and bachelor's degrees in textile management and teaching.

Lukas is the author of five previous books: *The Performance Triangle*, *Management Design*, *People-Centric Management*, *Agile by Choice* and *Diagnostic Mentoring*.